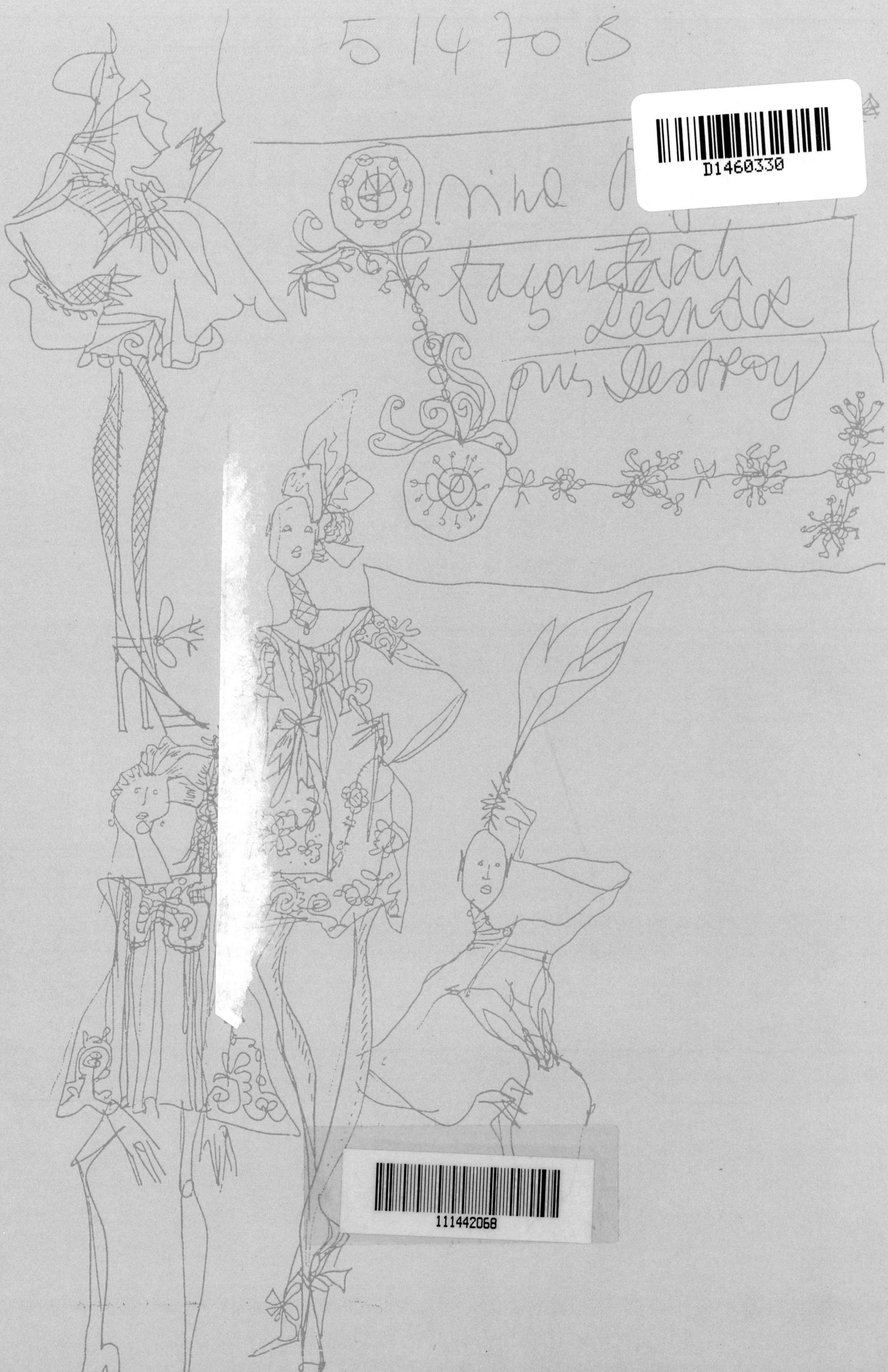

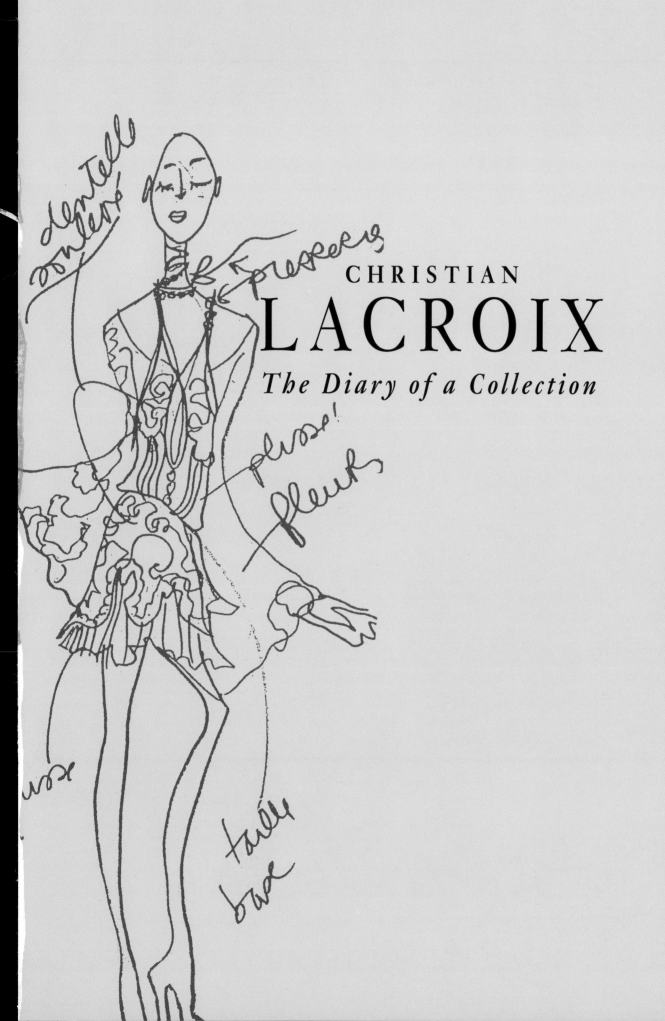

CHRISTIAN
LACROIX
The Diary of a Collection

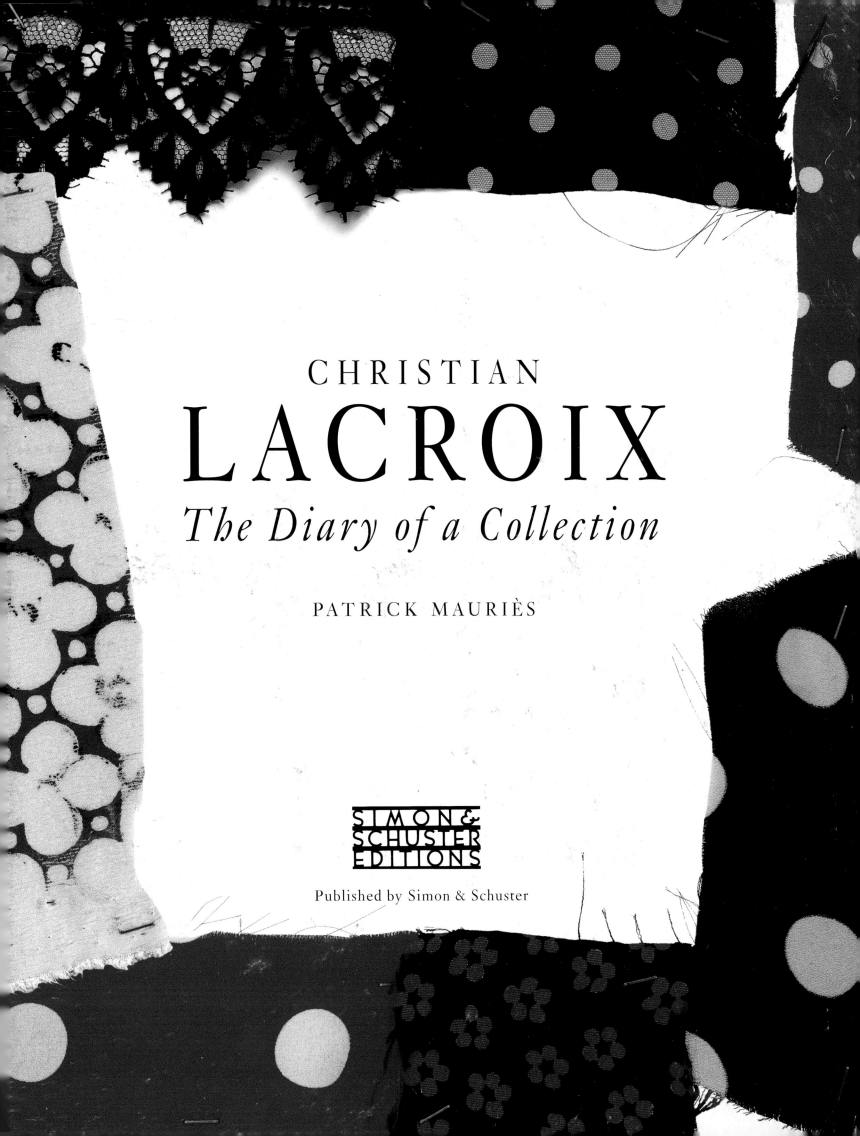

CHRISTIAN LACROIX

The Diary of a Collection

PATRICK MAURIÈS

SIMON & SCHUSTER EDITIONS

Published by Simon & Schuster

Anciens Monumens d'Arles en Provence,

Dédié à l'Académie Royale des Antiquaires de France

Par son très humble & obéissant

Translated from the French by Jane Brenton

SIMON & SCHUSTER EDITIONS
Rockefeller Center
1230 Avenue of the Americas
New York, New York 10020

First published in Great Britain by Thames and Hudson Ltd,
London

SIMON & SCHUSTER EDITIONS and colophon are
trademarks of Simon & Schuster Inc.

Designed and typeset by Thames and Hudson
Printed in Singapore by C.S. Graphics Pte Ltd

10 9 8 7 6 5 4 3 2 1

Library of Congress Cataloging in Publication Data

Mauriès, Patrick, 1952–
    Christian Lacroix : the diary of a collection / Patrick
    Mauriès.
        p.   cm.
    Includes index.
    ISBN 0–684–83259–3
    1. Costume design—France—History—20th century.
2. Costume design—France—History—20th century—
Pictorial works. 3. Fashion —France—History—20th
century.
4. Fashion—France—History—20th century—Pictorial
works. 5. Lacroix, Christian, 1951–
I. Title.
TT504.6.F7M38   1997
746.9'2'092—dc20   96-14908
                                                       CIP

CONTENTS

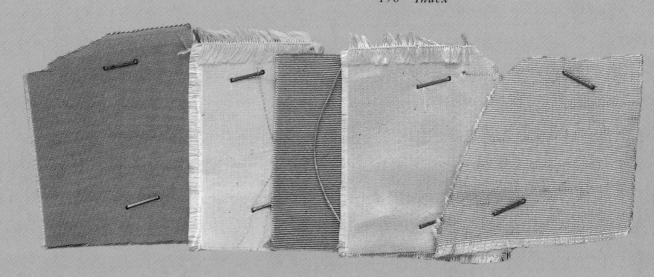

Before You Begin

Remember - this is a log-book. I started keeping a diary of the Haute-Couture Collection for Spring-Summer 96 at the suggestion of a friend. It begins with the first image, unexpected and enigmatic which whispered a somewhat hesitant "Eureka", and ends with the music of the finale which, following the applause, sends the parade back into the wings for ever.

I emphasize this because I am writing now more than 2 years after lighting upon these images. Fashion, like butterflies are born to die. Style on the other hand, is said to have the opposite destiny — to live for ever. I do not claim to make use of that term, nor would I wish to - it has no place here. What interested me was the kaleidoscope of "ideas", the day to day advances, the way the cogwheels engage with an almost spoke-like precision, so that a labyrinthine confusion of inspirations and insights ends up finally on the catwalk. The catwalk, the show, looks so coherent and assured, so superbly logical. But that season's wardrobe, shown in a mere thirty minutes, had occupied and preoccupied me for nearly three months, day and night. It is that process I have transmitted to Patrick Mauriès, taking it all to pieces in front of him.

Having done that, I now ask myself: is the mechanism always the same? Did subsequent Autumn, Winter and Spring collections follow the same rythm? or does the mechanism itself become outdated? Inevitably, the answer is equivocal. They were neither exactly the same nor completely different. Over the three seasons, the idea of adhering to a theme, a sort of trademark running through the work and picked up in the slogan adopted for the season, gave way to the search of a mood, an atmosphere, an attitude, something less artificially imposed but more nebulous, harder to pin down. Concrete illustration slid into abstract suggestion. The patchwork of alchemical anachronisms and geographical hybrids, happy accidents of all descriptions, is tending now to coalesce, as if subjected to centrifugal force into a subtle monochrome calligraphy, deadpan in mood. Clothes reflect the moment, as we know, but the moment can only be seen through the prism of a particular personality.

Every season has its own approach, and the diary of this particular journey offers merely one example. Or so it appears on the surface — deep down, no doubt they are all the same. You can try to transform the world, or at least the way it looks. What you cannot change is yourself. The child and the adolescent acquire a set of characteristics that become ingrained; the adult merely lives them out, or puts up with them. A designer, a creative artist, a couturier, will explore them and make them bear fruit. Which is only to say that, even if this scrapbook is now part of the past, it may yet serve as a passport to the other side of the looking glass.

A Couturier: The Creative Process

Christian Lacroix's previous book, *Pieces of a Pattern*, was without doubt an extraordinary work. Loosely based on the old English tradition of the scrapbook – a sort of homemade anthology – it attempted to bring together the elements of that mosaic of motifs which constitutes an individual's unique imaginative world, and to show how all these elements come together in the work of a famous designer (a creature who today is subject to such sophisticated marketing that it is sometimes hard to believe that he really exists).

It was *Pieces of a Pattern* which inspired American *Vogue* to ask several designers, and Christian Lacroix in particular, for a couple of pages of a real or fictitious scrapbook which illustrated the trends or keynotes of their next collection, that of January 1994.

Since Lacroix is not a man given to half measures, or maybe because the project touched a chord in him, his scrapbook grew to elephantine proportions. Behind the five or six

pages published in *Vogue* lay two huge volumes, two sketchbooks of grey-brown paper overflowing with images, samples, sketches, scraps of embossed leather and shot taffeta, gold paper crowns, Polaroids and pieces of lace.

Because these two volumes offer a unique insight into the working methods of one of today's leading designers – the development of a collection *over time*, the ripening of ideas, the technical aspects, even the hidden inspirations – we are reproducing them here almost in their entirety, accompanied by a brief explanation of what they contain.

No doubt there will be some mean spirits, self-professed cultural commentators or popular pundits, who insist that this is all a lot of fuss about nothing, that something so lightweight does not deserve this much attention; that it is yet another example of the confusion in values we are experiencing today, the way the established hierarchies and the boundaries between the genres are being blurred, lumping together 'high' and 'low', noble and popular forms in the manner that was so terribly fashionable under Structuralism and then Post-Modernism, but which has become outmoded now that the novelty has worn off, and people are returning to (or taking refuge in) traditional, canonical distinctions.

Our response to this is that it is always interesting and instructive to follow a mind at work; that despite appearances the jury is still out on the whole question of the established hierarchy of cultural values; and that fashion, both as regards its constituent elements and as an overall phenomenon, remains worthy of attention and analysis, and can teach us a good deal about the state of society and its choices and desires at any given moment. Moreover, we will get the same enjoyment from these pages as from seeing a puzzle fall into place or reading the pages of a private journal or workbook, tracing drafts and corrections, blinding illuminations and blind alleys, not to mention the aesthetic pleasure that is to be had from the collages themselves, the interplay of textures and colours, the dialogue between sketch and printed image, between the vitality of drawing and photography.

❖

We tend on the whole to have a rather prosaic idea of what a couturier actually does; we imagine that he dreams something up, produces a sketch, sends it to be made, assesses a three-dimensional version (a 'toile') of the design, makes modifications and corrections, sends it back, looks at it again and finally puts his name to a finished creation made of fabric and ready for the catwalk. Sketching, giving instructions, making alterations, these seem to be the essentials of a craft in which it is no longer customary to drape the model, as Madeleine Vionnet and Alix Grès used to do, and where the details of cut are no longer the be-all and end-all, as they were for Balenciaga and Charles James. (Although there are signs among the new generation of a return to this more tactile and technical interpretation of the art.)

Lacroix's approach is much more complex, so complex in fact that it has dictated the structure of this book, which is designed to reflect and illuminate his advances and hesitations at every step of the way.

He begins with a flash of inspiration, an insight, intuition or image that establishes the overall mood. This image simply emerges, imposes itself and takes over, for the prime characteristic of Lacroix's work is, paradoxically, the care he takes to avoid being in control: determined, once a particular direction has been chosen (or discovered), to explore all its ramifications and corollaries, its by-ways and diversions, multiplying, accumulating and stratifying the options and possibilities. What computer buffs call 'noise', but taken to the nth degree: a carefully maintained chaos or instability, out of which in due course the solution cannot but emerge. Because time – for gestation or for changes of heart – is the most precious commodity for a designer constantly faced with deadlines and delays, with the demands of the moment. And so he creates opportunities, encourages encounters, interactions, detours and accidents, 'puts all the balls in play'; it is the perfect approach for a mind that is – as we shall discover – always on the lookout for signs, coincidences and chance confirmations: like a gambler, or perhaps an oracle, practising something halfway between doodling and divination.

As we have already said, it was Lacroix's own approach that dictated the shape of this book. Nothing is less suited to generalization, to a textual overview, than his sort of haphazard progress from one surprise to the next, one accident to the next – one piece of cloth falling against another, an item of jewelry or a photograph brought in by an assistant, a letter in the post, something seen on television or in a newspaper, a sample in a range submitted by a supplier. All those tiny details that suddenly catch the eye, that are brought together, pushed apart, overlaid on one another, assembled over a long and fruitful period of gestation, call for patient, accurate careful commentary following along from one idea to the next, one image to the next. For there is a sense in which each Lacroix collection represents a sort of private diary kept by the designer, day by day, throughout the period of the run-up to the show.

✣

Time is an essential dynamic in Lacroix's work. As we know, he could just as well have been an art historian, and another aspect of his work reflects his fascination with the images of the past, the phantom signs that have the power to evoke times gone by. These scrapbook pages will make the exact nature of that preoccupation clear, should clarification be needed.

For there is nothing nostalgic or reverential or indeed retrograde in this passion for past eras. Lacroix was born in the fifties, at one of those rare moments in history when 'modernization' – new techniques, the quiet dismantling of old forms – was accepted as wholly good, the means of leaving the ravages of war behind and moving to a bright, happy future. So he belongs to that generation which gradually succeed-ed in abolishing the strict antithesis between old and new, which was able to recover its heritage and claim for itself, among other forbidden delights, the taste for ornament, for texture and volume, for materials rejected by the 'progressive' orthodoxies, and to find a new way of using this vocabulary, this treasure that was suddenly made available again.

The past consists of multiple realities and fleeting insights and is important only in respect of what it liberates, the things it reveals or makes clear, the shock of seeing with new eyes: a piece of faded material discovered in one of those legendary English country houses, on a parasol left abandoned in the sunshine of childhood, or in a detail of a dress glimpsed in a museum. One pole of a dynamic, one element of a collage, is justified by the interaction it sets up, the way it resonates with the other elements, and also with contemporary needs, in this way becoming incorporated – with all its uncertainties, insecurities and obscurities – directly into the present.

For the collection whose progress is recorded here, 'present' means the end of 1993, and the period leading up to the haute couture show held in January 1994. That time is of intrinsic historical interest insofar as the collection marked one of those significant moments when the history of modern fashion took a new turn. Lacroix put it succinctly when he described his inspiration as a 'return to the eighties'. For several seasons fashion had in its own way reflected the general crisis affecting society. Drawing in its horns, and making much of its supposed austerity, it had turned its back on baroque excess, the 'indecent' extravagance and 'nouveau-riche' embellishments that were the obvious symbols of the easy money, get-rich-quick attitudes of the previous decade. But what it also eliminated were the frivolity and theatricality that are among the essential attributes of fashion and of Lacroix's designs in particular. As a result of this prevailing ethos, as he tells us himself, he had stopped showing the exuberant and expensive 'showpiece' dresses, which he had been the first to reintroduce in 1987 (does this situation perhaps compare with the scandalized reaction to the enormous amount of fabric needed to create the New Look in the immediate postwar years?).

The following pages show (and herein lies their interest to the fashion historian) how Lacroix sensed the earliest signs of this new direction, the 'revival of elegance' and search for 'glamour' which is in full swing today. A trailblazer in this respect, he has always held to the idea of fashion as indivisible and uncompromising, an activity involving contributions from people in many different crafts, with different expertise and skills, and he has tended to blur the distinction between *prêt-à-porter* and couture – often being criticized for doing so – because he cannot abide second-best or watered-down versions. For him, the essence of his craft consists in extravagant and splendidly useless gestures, as well as that slow and painstaking approach that is so much at variance with the speed of modern life. Today there is a whole school of design that, in its turn, defends the concept of fashion as a splendid artifice, which produces clothes whose perfection requires immaculate fitting, the precision of a watchmaker and unjustifiably long hours of work. In this we may see the confirmation of that intransigence with which Lacroix has clung to his belief in flamboyant display, characterized by elegance and lightness of touch, shot through with memories and history, playful and bright, cosmopolitan and Parisian – couture which shows life for what it often forgets it really is: a theatre.

~1~

Memories, Quests and Encounters

4–5   The print displayed in the entrance lobby, which you vaguely notice in the morning and in the evening as you go in or out with your mind on the day's post or the meeting you are about to go to, is the one you tracked down in Montpellier and hung carefully in this prominent position as a symbol. It acts as a sign or a quiet statement to anyone entering the premises, for subsumed within this single image are the monuments of Arles, the personal landscape that means so much to you. A landscape of ruins and relics in an imaginary panorama, it is a prescient blend of dream and reality, things real and things remembered.

  The print is here in this book thanks to one of those moments when, for no particular reason, ordinary things that familiarity has rendered invisible take on a new clarity. You suddenly noticed, towards the bottom of the picture, tiny figures moving about, three nineteenth-century sightseers moving graciously among the ruins. The woman was wearing one of those low-necked, high-waisted dresses, made of lightweight materials falling in long folds, that aspired (presciently?) to recreate the myth of Ancient Greece. This was to be your point of departure, the germ of the idea for a new collection.

❖

This print, *The Monuments of Arles*, is itself a fictional representation 34–35 of the past, an impossible reinvention of the marvels of antiquity. For Christian Lacroix there was no question of quoting literally something that was itself a collage of quotations. Although never indifferent to the appeal of the past, he is always aware that he is addressing the present, responding to its conscious and unconscious needs. What appeared to him, like a ghost, in a single pictorial detail, was an initial silhouette, a line, which had the merit of further 'legitimizing' the references to the South of France that are a constant (and often misinterpreted) theme in his work: the traditional costume of the women of Arles had roughly the same proportions as the elegant Directoire frock; it was like one of those optical illusions – as one image melted away, the other replaced it. The duality avoided the trap of mere imitation; it 'modernized' the South of France theme.

This first discovery leads directly to the second, or at least to the recollection of it: a theatrical jacket unearthed one day in the 34 fabulous Rastro – the Madrid flea market – a place that was a source of endless fascination for Ramón Gómez de la Serna, and the subject of an extraordinary treatise by him. (A remarkable essayist and author of unclassifiable texts somewhere on the boundaries between philosophical reflection and psychological analysis, personal confession and fiction, Gómez de la Serna could not have failed to be interested in flea markets – places of exchange, of interaction between past and present.) Certain features of this black jacket, probably nineteenth-century, will be heard of again later – the distinctive cut, the square buttons, the curious way the sleeve is bent at the elbow.

✛

Initial sketches and jottings: in 1994, we commemorated the landings of the Allies on French beaches, so the memory of the forties was very much alive. It is impossible to underestimate that decade's influence on the fashions of today. Like the end of the eighteenth century, it was one of those periods of instability that particularly fascinated Lacroix, a time of transition between two eras, two cultures, a time of things completed and things left unresolved. Another fragment of the mosaic thus fell into place as one of the typical motifs of that period was pressed into service – those printed fabrics whose particular quality and flavour seemed synonymous with wartime uncertainties.

Again, there was something of the flea market about all this: shoulder-pads, tired crêpes-de-chine, plastic powder compacts, platform shoes, all the paraphernalia we fell on with cries of joy in the seventies and which for Lacroix as for anyone else of his generation remained indissolubly linked with that period. The kaleidoscope endlessly shakes its pieces, the images are superimposed, from the eighteenth century to the 1940s, to the seventies, and from the seventies to the present day. Here are some pictures by Guy Bourdin, from *Nova*, one of those magazines now long since 39 disappeared that are not so much a part of history as of our memories; they drift in the limbo of our personal lives and are suddenly recollected. Here, too, are photographs by Francesco Scavullo, who, with Helmut Newton and Bourdin, was the 42, 49 iconographer of the age, the person whose style most closely corresponded to the times, to the point that his layout, his poses, the quality of his light, as well as the models' actual physique and make-up, immediately call up the precise feel of the period, with its fascination with flamboyant masquerade.

There are no 'logical' connections between these reminiscences of a recent past characterized by pleasure and excess (at Studio 54 in New York, at the Club Sept in Paris) and the other elements of the mix; what Lacroix retained above all of the former was a particular quality of glamour, make-up and presentation; it helped him to get rid of the strictly historical connotations of the Directoire line and to avoid the pitfalls of imitation.

⊹

This eighteenth-century bonnet holds the eye less because of its form 44–45 (or function) than because of its *textures* – a fascinating complexity of ruches, pleats and frills, a network of pintucks, overlappings and insertions – and its indefinable blond colour (natural, perhaps, or the colour of time itself, beyond calculation). It presupposes an extraordinary skill and exquisite workmanship which simply do not exist today, and that is part of its fascination; it also exactly complements the grey-brown colour and the design of a dress of 1880-1900, with its insertions, its transparencies and opacities, that attractive blend of outright prettiness and severe fabric. Lacroix, furthermore, has always had a weakness for see-through effects, for example the play of hollows and solids in a piece of lace – a seductive material because it suggests lingerie, undergarments, bodily intimacy, and because, once again, it is taken out of context and worn on the outside, holding in place a veil of muslin or some other flowing fabric.

This precious object from the past, this bonnet, turns into a sort of rhetorical figure such as the semiologists would have been proud of. As element or accessory, it is indispensable; as a part, it contributes materially to the whole; and, metaphysically, it provides the inspiration for an entire and very special dress (noted down in the quick sketch at the foot of the page). Evolution, adaptation and expansion of the basic idea . . . three fundamental elements of the creative process.

❖

46–47 The limited colour combinations used for daywear (lifted, incidentally, straight from the seventies) seem the very model of economy and expressiveness, a rational and planned use of resources in the face of technical constraints and the limitations of mass production: apart from the 'non-colours' – black and white – the only colour used was a simple plain red. Prints are a special case, the aim in general being to do more with less, the same colour range running through from design to finished fabric. But here the clock is turned back to a different era, the ghost that appears to Lacroix is dressed in the summer fashions of his childhood, simple frocks with defined waists, leg-of-mutton or short sleeves, in flowing, lightweight fabrics, with high necks or peter-pan collars. Though these styles date back to the forties, their influence lived on in the provinces (where innovation was suspect and quiet self-restraint the norm) right up to the sixties; then they vanished, along with those superb hats that were also still being worn, with variations to suit the occasion.

Here is another proof of the extent to which fashion is a matter of coincidences and chance encounters: a Swedish colleague thought Lacroix might be interested in a photograph of ladies at the court in Stockholm, in which the protagonists wear the obligatory uniform of dark dress with lace collar and, notably, the slashed sleeves reminiscent of the Empire style. This divided fabric, the same ripped, laddered effect, cropped up again out of the blue – in a striking fashion detail which anticipated the frenzies of punk and grunge – in an uncannily prophetic photograph by Scavullo. And, as if that were not enough, the chenille weaving samples by Ulrika Liljedahl arrived at the very same moment. Various different expressions of the one idea – crocheted and frayed cloth, coarse mesh with flesh or lining showing through, contrasting with the delicate effect of lace – which

48–49

was to feature in the sleeves of one of the showpiece dresses in the final parade.

✤

As we know, many different crafts come together in couture, each working at its own speed, its proper tempo. Here we have two quick 51 sketches of shoes, literally poles apart, both of which were made up in the form shown: one 'tasteful', with 'cottonreel' heels, picking up on the idea of fin-de-siècle lacework ; the other 'risqué', combining two incompatibles, the stiletto heel and the trainer, common currency of streetwear and emblem of middle-ranking fashion for all.

But the very first thing that must be considered is the embroidery, that hallmark of Lacroix's couture. Exquisite brocades, damascene work, braiding and overstitching, giving the fabric thickness and texture – all additional handwork: the patient, caressing process of designing, fashioning and sculpting the precious surface, with that impossibly time-consuming attention to exquisite detail that can only be justified by the ruinously high cost and equally high expectations of haute couture.

The master-embroiderer must of course be given a rough idea or outline of the theme he will have to develop. Lacroix works with one of the oldest embroidery houses in the capital. François Lesage, its proprietor, has fought to protect his unique heritage with all its accumulated experience. He introduced himself to Lacroix in 1982, at Patou. Amazed at the workmanship on offer, Lacroix must have thought of Lesage as his fashion godfather, and himself as the favoured godson. The collaboration between the two has continued since then, always very much as a two-way exchange. Lesage prepares his own collection with his own themes, in which the couturier tries to reserve a few models exclusively for him; and sometimes it is Lacroix who suggests a particular idea or motif.

Here we can see an example of their collaboration, centring on an 54–55, 56–57 embroidered picture of the Virgin dating from the eighteenth century, which Lesage had given to Lacroix sometime earlier. This became overlaid with a Polish devotional folk image, and with memories of elaborate ex-voto offerings in the rustic tradition, exhibiting the same blend of extreme sophistication and a refinement that would be in-conceivable today (openwork like a spider's web, near-invisible looping threads) with 'primitive' crudeness and clumsiness, a combination that has always fascinated Lacroix. It supplied the inspiration for Lesage's contribution, masterly as ever, to the last item in the show: the texture and motifs of the Virgin's triangular-petalled rose – though in a reverse image, as befits translations and transliterations – were incorporated into the bodice of the wedding gown of the season.

⁙

Glittering water and crystals; that was the colour note Lacroix gave for the embroidery. It was a new development in his use of colour, enriching the spectrum of bright Southern tones with which his name had become linked. The trend would become increasingly marked over succeeding collections: a range of colours arrived at instinctively, but at the same time playing with the notion of 'faded brilliance': glorious, strong colours, but bleached out like the fabric of a parasol used too long in the sun.

This muted colouring amounted to a further restatement of the collection's forties theme. Lacroix was given further confirmation that he was on the right track when he visited the Lesage archives in the Rue de la Grange-Batelière, a fascinating little room where all their creations – including those from the forties – have been stored away, season by season, since the nineteenth century. (Here Lacroix also saw those subtle blends of, for example, fibre, hair and plastic that were perfectly acceptable then, though they still seem hugely daring even today.) It was in the tweeds in particular that he looked for that precise shade of colour found in very early Kodachrome photographs or in mid-century films. This was colour that did not exist at any other time; it made a lasting impression on a few generations and then disappeared with them. It was the colour of film matinées, in big old-fashioned provincial cinemas with plasterwork décor, matinées that were broken by an interval which was punctuated by the slight creak of wicker baskets loaded with ices and sweets carried by the usherettes. With its distinctive bluey greys, deep reds, soft greens and yellows, and its sooty black, this was not the colour of real life. Eventually it disappeared, as technical progress moved towards an ever more transparent and hallucinatory effect of realism.

Nostalgia for these subtle shades has been one of Lacroix's constant underlying preoccupations, and, however little you might expect it, there is actually something rather poignant about this search for an elusive palette of colours (as precise as that of the Greeks or Romans, whose ideas of black and white remain a closed book to us) that is bound up with his memories.

÷

Lacroix was also working on the cut or structure of a jacket: old books 58–59 were consulted, following up the idea of the Rastro coat – sleeves bent at the elbow, close-fitting over the shoulders and body: it needed a fairly stiff fabric but one that was flexible as well as resistant. Lacroix had previously picked up in London's Portobello Road a sort of Oriental shawl in bronze and écru tones, made of muslin and silk; he gave this to Anne Corbière, and, using it as her inspiration, she wove silk in the style of raffia matting to create a smooth, stiff cloth, the colour of sunlight.

Lacroix had first met Anne Corbière through a theatrical adaptation of Goethe's *Wilhelm Meister* in the late 1980s. As with Lesage, the collaboration is very much a two-way affair, a matter of suggestions and interpretations, trials and adjustments. So the silk shawl was turned into something heavy and substantial, but through the use of superb dyeing techniques the faded colour of the original was retained.

The theatre, the Rastro, Portobello Road, long-vanished townhouse attics, all are scenes of encounters with memory – the memories of the past, both recent times, as of the Sunday market in Arles to which Lacroix went with his parents, and of past ages. A store of treasures overflowing with *objets trouvés* that are important in the designer's eyes not because of their rarity – he is in no sense a collector – but for what they arouse or provoke in him, for their metaphorical and imaginative power: as we see, a mere detail of fabric or cut may become part of a new conundrum, a whole new creation.

❖

64–65 Behind these flowing white dresses of airy muslin, persisting behind this sweet, old-fashioned silhouette (like an object remaining on the retina) is the Directoire line; a look at Barbier and Lepape's designs is enough to put the matter beyond doubt. But a fashion like this is not so much 'what grandmother used to wear', as a matter of its echoes, in the careful copies of Visconti, the free interpretations of Fellini. These belong to the seventies as much as to the forties; and superimposed on Visconti's nostalgia for his own childhood is our nostalgia for a wonderful and unique moment of cinema. More routinely, the line is also echoed in the sets and costumes of television programmes mimicking in their own way the attributes of this age of elegance. Tulles, satins and lace are never innocent; they release whole swathes of memories, insubstantial ghosts and recollections.

❖

You never entirely forget the moment when you first chose your own clothes, when you took on the responsibility for what you buy, how you wear it and how you look – and the fashion of that moment remains somehow in the back of your mind as Fashion with a capital F, in a state of improbable perfection. For Lacroix that moment occurred around 1972, when people were happily mixing prints, spots and stripes, taking the thirties as their example. This is why the seventies crops up so frequently in his collections. As another example of chance encounters: he was struck by the mix-and-match use of pattern, vaguely patchwork in feel, in a photograph by Michel Dieuzaïde of an old Spaniard; at the same time he came 67 across a series of printed fabrics at Gandini's that might have been based on the photograph. Here we can see the three elements of the creative process coming together: the image that 'clicks', unpredictably and out of the blue; the range of fabric samples produced and submitted by the manufacturers, which will either fit that first idea or not; and the design of the garment, conceived with no thought of constraints or parameters, and which will or will not accord with the above. (In this particular case, the finished garment turns out in the end to be neither 'Spanish' nor 'ethnic', but rather more eighteenth-century in feel.)

And there are private references, too: leaving a fashion exhibition 68 at the Metropolitan Museum of Art in New York, Lacroix noticed three tiny hourglass-shaped busts dating from the 1880s. On closer inspection he found that they were made of jersey embroidered with jet; this amazingly modern combination of textures is to be translated wholesale into an embroidered bodice used in the show.

At first glance there appears to be nothing in common between the super-modern brightly coloured synthetic outfit worn by a

70–71   motorcycle racer and the linings of Provençal garments, left lying

purely by chance next to the open page of a book on motor-

cycling. And yet the eye quickly establishes a visual connection,

and another could legitimately be made at a deeper level, for these

are both working garments; the linings of the clothes used day to

day in Provence are made of scraps and remnants for reasons of

economy, while the clothes of today's bikers reflect a deep

lack of unity, the bright pleasure-

seeking brashness of modern life.

So these are two examples of

fashion reflecting life, forerunners

of streetwear, fashion to be worn as

well as seen in.

Arles en Provence,
Antiquaires de France,
Par son très humble & obéissant Serviteur

...tiquity + DIRECTOIRE = 90?

ATLAS Antique III

1980

antistyle anti-modern
anti-cliché

dandy
anglo
provencal

Boléro
cf
← livre
anglais

SUPER
POSITION
de ???
antistyle
et de
matelas
-sages pro-
-vençaux

← essayer
matelassé
provençal
d'été
d'aspect
transparent

robes diaphanes.

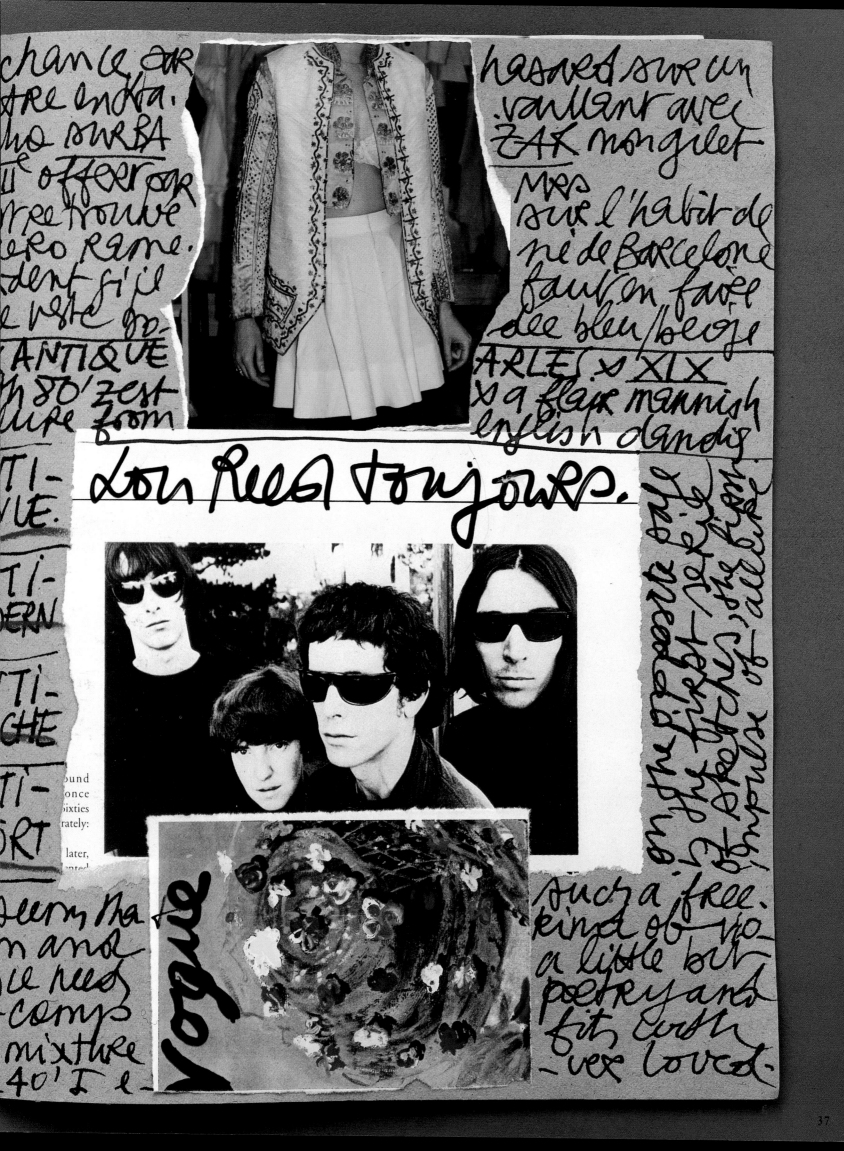

Lou Reed toujours.

Vogue

tacky fashion of TV music programs

DIRECTOIR

e same lightness and dARING style

premières

Têtes

de

coiffures

dernier fashionnable

iRECTOIRE MEETS WITH THE MID 70'
ND LATE 80 OR EARLY 90 BLACK STYLE
INS WHITE SHEER AUDACITY TROUGH LYCRA

ces trois images sont la même femme

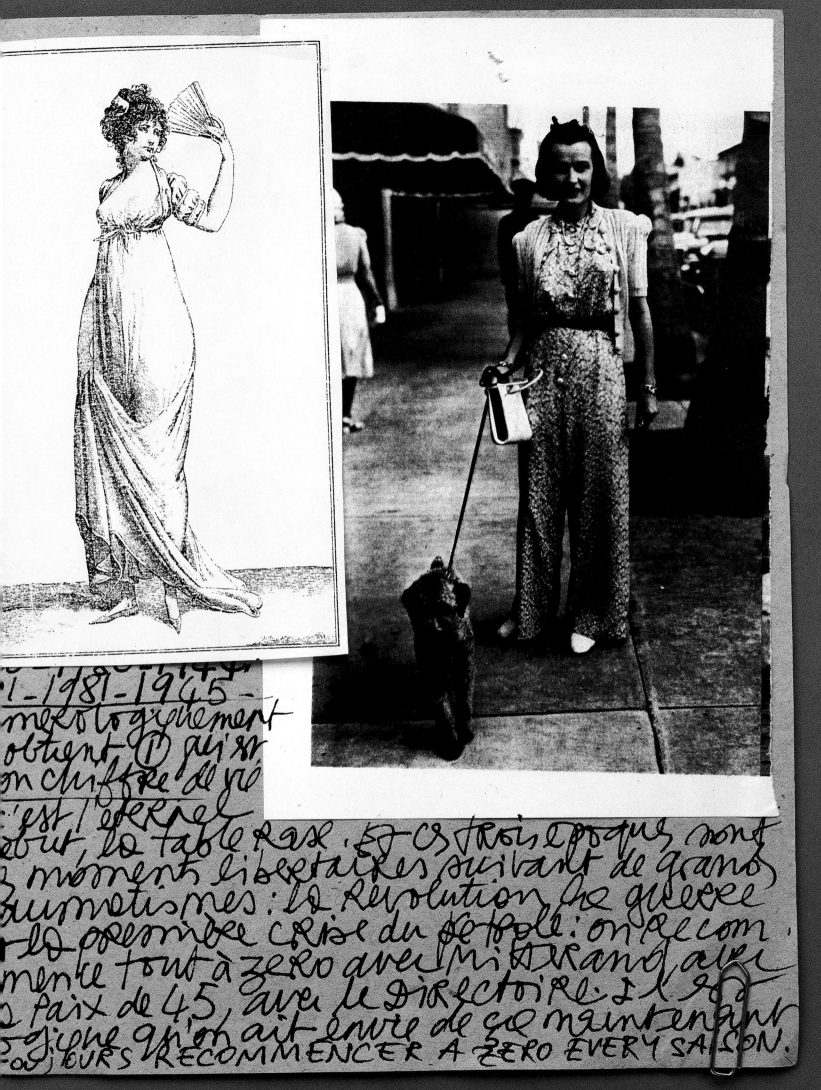

1-1981-1945-
nécrologiquement
obtient ① qui se
n chiffre de ye
'est l'éternel
ebut, la table rase. Et ces trois époques sont
moments libertaires suivant de grands
aurmatismes: la Révolution, la guerre
la première crise du pétrole: on recom-
mence tout à zéro avec Mitterand, avec
faix de 45, avec le Directoire. Il se
que qu'on ait envie de ce maintenant
oujours RECOMMENCER A ZERO EVERY SAISON.

43

Bonnet provençal du XVIIIe

envie de travaux très couture : per vues
entre-deux, plissés bijoux, dentelle blonde
Tout ça n'est pas
couture

juxtaposer raffinement naïveté et tissus bruts

Jacques Heim. Legroux Sœurs
Crêpe de chine vert et blanc de Ducharne

Francevramant. Legroux Sœurs
Crêpe de chine noir et blanc de Combier

Mad Carpentier. Agnès
Crêpe de chine à pois de Ducharne

Maggy Rouff. Legroux Sœurs
Crépon noir à pois jaunes de Couturier

Molyneux
Dessin de cannage gris et blanc

Lucien Lelong. Rose Valois
Rayures noires, vertes et blanches sur crêpe

lle Dormoy. Suzy
de Ducharne

Jacques Heim
Crêpe bordeaux et blanc

Envie de ce genre d'imprimés fleuris

envie de ce genre de l'honnêtes fe

Schiaparelli
Pingouins rouge et blanc sur noir de Ducharne

24

Le costume d'apparat de la cour de suède en 1940/1950 est une évolution du costume Empire (Ls manches)

ention aux faux
nks aussi stupides
e le grunge. Mais le
aussures sont in
essantes er la maill
jornt les essais sal
chenilles d'Ulrika,
DE SUEDE, cuir - cuir

LACROIX

49

TOUS LES PIEDS JERONT OR

pourquoi pas de roches

↓ 1910 ↓

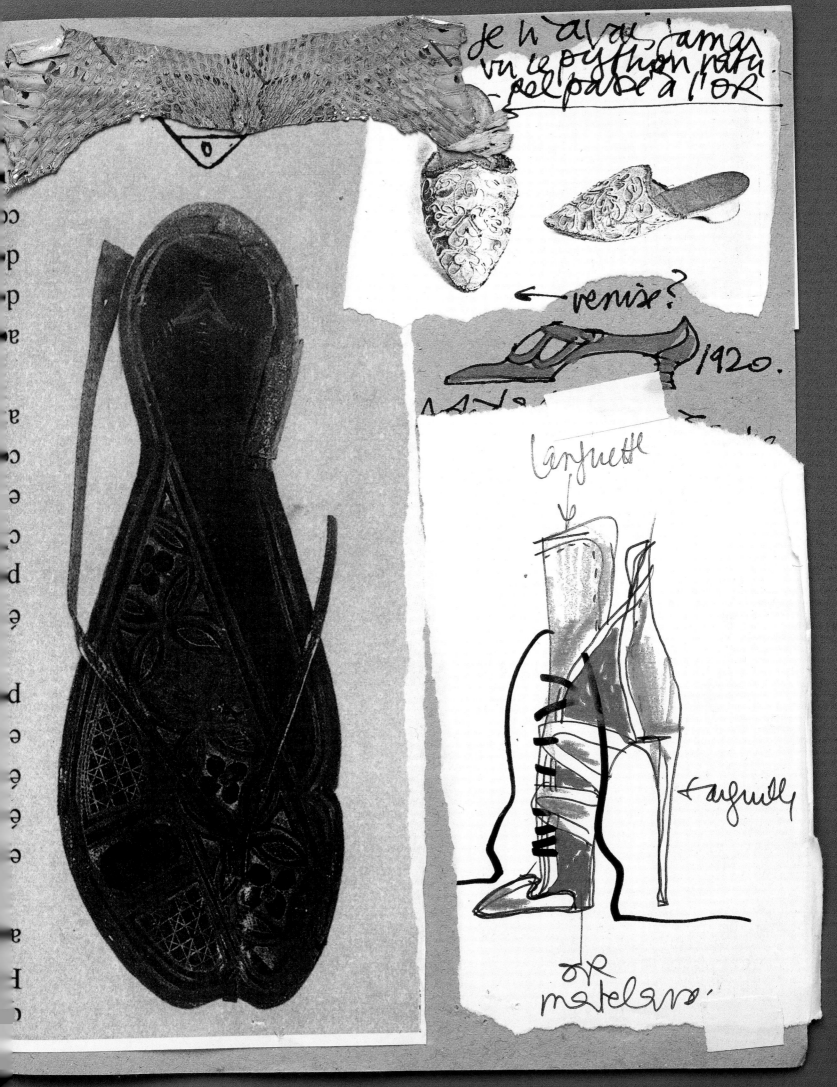

je n'avai jama
vu le python natu.
rel pose a l'OR

venise?   1920.

languette

aiguille

matelasse

LACROIX

REPORTAGE PAMELA DIEU PHOTOS JEAN-DENIS MAHN

80

A faire essa sir chez LeBourget et Dasso.

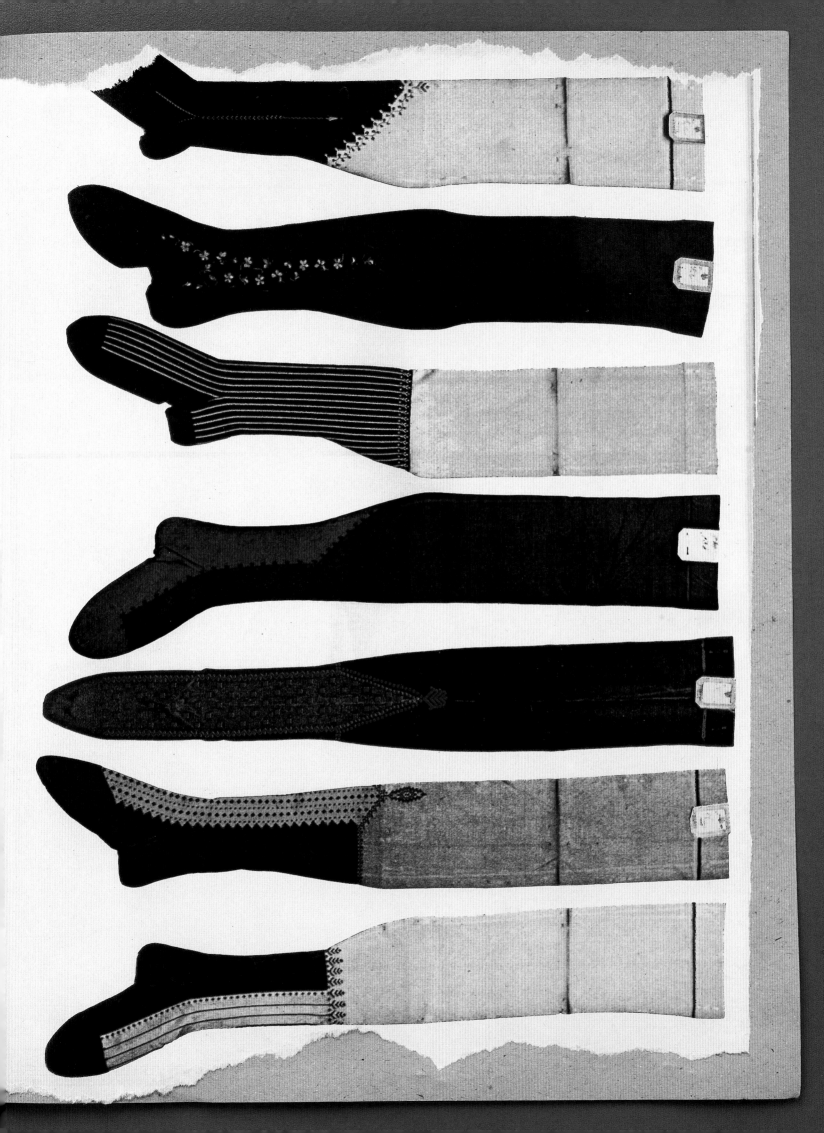

CONSOLATRIX ... PRO NOBIS

GLORIOSA VIRGO MARIA MATER IESU
CONSOLATRIX AFFLICTORUM
Patrona Civitatis et Patriæ Luxemburgensis in Sacello
Soc. IESV Miraculis Clara.

Enfant Jesus
Jupe pourrait
le Marié -
trop theatre
Mai finale.
Couture
que jamais
reserve
que j'aime
tendre.

polonais: la
deverre elle d
Attention au
ou trop opera
-ment en
on doit fle
alles par
res
par ce
san

Retrouver le livres d'Sr. Victor de

Mais preuse saint Sulpice
m'angrant dentelle et couleurs vives.

documents anciens à Évelyne.
TISSAGE ANNE CORBIERE À PARTIR D'UNE
ECHARPE RAMENEE DE PORTOBELLO en septembre

la forme, la proportion et le mélange de tissus sont plus que contemporain. Ne pas hésiter à commencer.

Finely worked buttonholes on the cuffs and for the front opening, as well as the skillful tailoring of the body and sleeves, attest to the maker's talent as well as the owner's wealth.

The weave in this garment is known as "bizarre" and consists of a fanciful pattern of gold and silver threads with pink silk damask in the upper back and upper sleeves.

Men of the eighteenth century wore waistcoats such as this elaborate article (1705–20).

34

59

IX
93

nois de choix tissus ?

TAFFETAS
CHAINE
ROUGES
JAUNE

Pour

chocolat. Tournesol - vermillon
bordeaux. pourpre. soufre. ciel
merise - violet → gamme
(georgette)

pastellissime, noir noury en
(satin douri ou né)

et en PS douppienne → effets
corset

douppion :
merise. noir - moutarde - violet
gamme

point de départ de la gamme noir
à l'instinct. livré de pastels acids
et de vifs un peu passés, usés.

drapier

dentelle ; imprimés/bracelets

on a fait un es
mots de bonbons
africains

exclusifs à faire
Attention à ce que
tt le monde ne fait
pas.

Finalement non

61

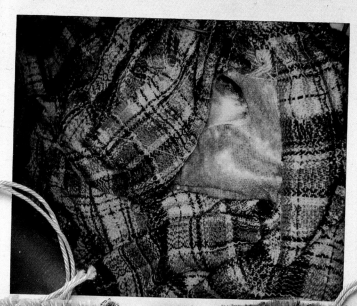

58–9 Pourpoint worn by Charles of Blo[is]
[L]yon, Musée Historique des Tissus. (Mus[ée]

...is, back and [fr]ont view. Before 1364.
[fro]m phot[o]

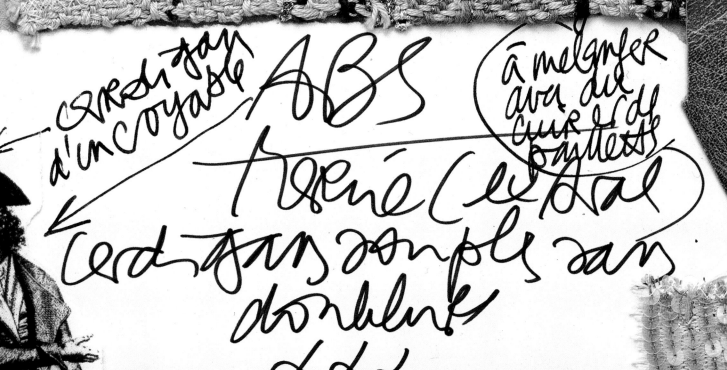

cardigan d'incroyable

ABS

à mélanger avec du cuir et de paillettes

René Cristal

c'est très ample sans doublure

LLL

Envie de barrer les robes blanches trop
l'Effrei Romantique par une croix
de velours noir. (Trouver une ma-
-tière plus, été.). Toujours la MORT À
VENISE depuis toujours, les mélanges de
tulle et satin des heroïnes 1914 et
LA NAVE VA – Jouer sur
les superpositions un peu
inattendues – Broderies
légères dont on devrait
pouvoir les garder sans
doublure (impossible
pour les clientes) – Regar-
-der les images plus récen-
-tes Variétés Mixtie et
gilbert Carpentier sur
Canal Jimmy.) les
robes Disco de Dalida.
Fluidité un peu cheap et
paillettes Rejoignent à
la fois les reconstitutions
historiques 40, les robes
de tango ou celles d'Irène
Castle 1917 et bien sûr
les merveilleuses des
Palais Royal. 1800.

LACROIX

Regarder des images plus récentes de gitans
et de l'Espagne. Regarder d'un autre
œil les livres de photo achetés dans les
années 80 comme Scarullo. Ces années
là viennent de basculer dans le patri-
moine historique. On a trouvé de beaux/nouveaux
essais masculins (Gardizi, Sorimeine et
Ronana Schekye) : graphismes 75 de
magnereaux 1730 ou XVIIIe Jos Beaude

BIJOUX GRAPHIQUES ARGENT DE PANAMA

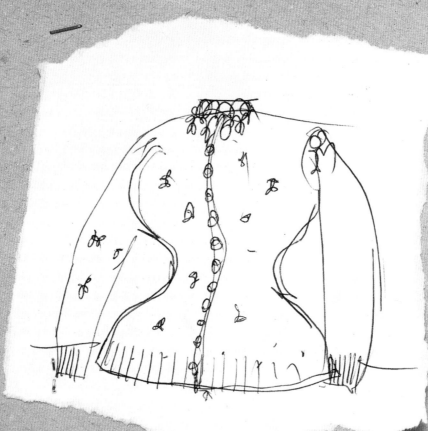

Vu à New York au metropolitan Muse
à la porté de l'exposition sur le show
des designers americain, à Versaille
en 1973. 3 buste minuscule en forme
de sablier 1880. Vu de près, on aperço
que c'est de la maille jersey avec bord
cote et tout bazde te fais — incroyable
dej de faire la même chose avec tanie
bontard en jersey de soie de Racine à
broder de fleurs (Isabela?) comme
de Chine XII
pulls cheap

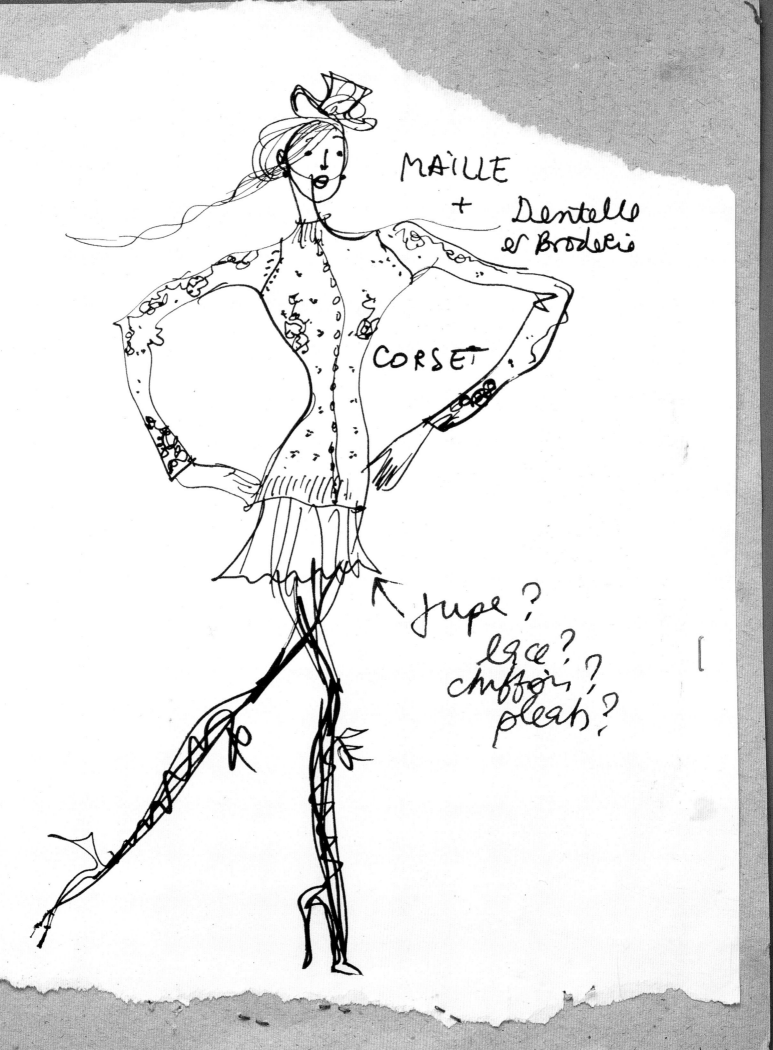

MAILLE
+
Dentelle
et Broderie

CORSET

↖ jupe?
lace?
chiffon?
pleats?

69

...mer en pleine ascension, ne ...onner la réplique tant sa maîtise est parfaite. ...comme à son habitude, à chaque fois qu'il a été titré, Jordi l'a été à l'avant dernier GP de la saison, et ce coup-ci, c'était en Finlande, sur les terres d'Ahvala, le vaincu de la saison. Il faut savoir que Jordi aime fêter ses titres en même temps que son anniversaire, le 10 septembre... Et maintenant, il totalise la bagatelle de cinq titres mondiaux, un record qui n'est pas près d'être atteint. N'empêche que malgré ce palmarès en or massif, Jordi n'a pas pu réprimer une larme d'émotion et de joie à la fin de la course qui le couronnait une nouvelle fois. On ne s'y habitue donc jamais ? Mais le pire, c'est que l'an prochain, à 27 ans, il fait encore figure de grandissime favori. Un immense champion...

...avec trois titres ...ours sur Beta, mais en 92, ...blèmes avec le constructeur italien ...erait pas attendre : il sera vice-champion, ...ar Ahvala et surtout il quitte Beta pour Gas Gas. Et, à l'orée de cette saison 93, au guidon de la moto espagnole, il commence par impressionner son monde par un campagne hivernale d'indoors qui en dit long sur sa forme et sa motivation. Et les premiers GP ne feront que confirmer cet état de fait : Jordi est bel et bien le plus fort.

~2~

By Chance and by Design

The second act, the heart of the action. Now comes the cornerstone of the whole edifice: the sketches, with their dual function of recording initial inspirations and looking ahead to the finished garments. The drawings made in preparing a collection are of two kinds. First, the rough outlines, more a sort of limbering up, where the hand (like the mind) experiments, feels its way and tries out all the possibilities, but is not yet really on course.

This process of aimless meandering is necessarily cut short, for in two or three days of intense graphic activity the essential identity of the collection has to be established and noted down. After this the hand moves on to explore and develop the theme and to follow its implications through. It is often at this point that the model pops up that will prove to be the star of the show, the bestseller; also (perhaps because of some unconscious desire for symmetry) the one used at intervals throughout the presentation. (Anyone who writes or sketches knows that creativity is often just the difficult matter of covering the distance between two poles, between a starting point and a conclusion that have presented themselves readymade, more or less out of the blue.)

'Disproportion'. This is the watchword of the collection, writ large 82
and in capital letters. Disproportion, or playing with scale: couture

surrendered to the whims of an evil genius, who exaggerates blouses to the point where they become dresses, pares down jackets and fitted coats to the shape of a bolero (our old friend from the Rastro putting in another appearance). These deliberate errors of perspective and sly changes of focus are to be one of the season's key statements. The Directoire theme provides the inspiration for the collars or high-necked blouses; while that period's counterpart, the forties, resurfaces in the flowing silks and the particular quality of the prints – another happy accident that provides confirmation of the theme.

❖

84–85   The sketching continues. Three times, inexplicably, the same silhouette appears. The hand obeys its own instinct (wiser than all the calculations of logic) and takes charge. A figure in profile, haughty bearing, walking, leg bent. Short hair, quiff or kiss-curl. Fitted coat/blazer, skimpy little jacket or flounced dress, the first with incongruous Adidas brocade shoes. Of these three possibles, the one on the left is to end up on the stage, while the one on the right will never get beyond the drawing board, because of technical limitations. Yet all three are essentially only sketches, born out of the contact between pencil or pen and paper; little try-out pieces that are barely deliberate, a sort of automatic writing enabling Lacroix to introduce an element of the unexpected and avoid the trap of uninspired planning and creeping rationalization.

The dress in the centre represents a new variation on the flowing line, but here the fluidity is meant to act as a foil: the spotted motif is supposed to stand out in quite marked contrast and relief against the lightweight muslin or silk. In the event it was to prove technically impossible to use patches of quilting on such delicate fabrics. It was not until later that Lacroix remembered where this idea might have come from (it was a curtain found in the Midi, which used this raised technique); his hand recollected it before he did.

In the same way as painting has its genres, from the most humble to the most exalted, and there are three types of discourse, so fashion too is pitched at different levels, ranging from the sublime to the vulgar. Astonishing though it may seem, in the era when music travels around the global village and we enjoy a classless society, fashion, or at least the firms who deal in it, seems to cling ferociously to some notion of what is appropriate or 'correct', even as that concept dwindles away in the rest of life. It is as though fashion were some ultimate luxury, or show, which has to be preserved at all costs in an outdated world that is on the brink of disappearing. And one, of course, where major investments are in the balance, and there is a duty – imposed by some parody of the superego – not to upset the average buyer, since he represents the yardstick by which everything else must be measured.

Lacroix is famous for his love of the theatrical, for the extravagance of his vision, and for his almost insatiable passion for the magic of couture. Nevertheless, he has always taken any opportunity to puncture its pretensions and attack its monolithic and inflexible nature: he would be the first to criticize the 'good' taste, the codified

elegance of a world where money supplies the code. So it is
appropriate that the central theme of this collection has to do with
disruption of scale, with reducing and exaggerating the sizes of
things. Shrunken-looking fitted coats, skimpy jackets that look as if
the wearer has outgrown them – a further evocation of the seventies
when the now sadly neglected photographer Guy Bourdin presented
85 his dramatic and sophisticated images, wide trousers with skinny
children's sweaters (which we see here embellished with gold thread,
the luxury of the texture providing a contrast).

The line was further enhanced by other references lifted outside their usual context: the ostentatious elegance of the 'Rasta', tight suits in rather stiff fabric in 'vulgar' white, a colour that is like a breath of fresh air in the middle-of-the-road culture of dark suits and discreet shades. In the end the problem remained as to how to adjust the hems to avoid lumpy double seams, and the outfit had to be made in beige. Instead of the planned waistcoat there was a T-shirt, which Lacroix originally imagined in Lycra, echoing the sporty theme, but which ended up in velvet etched with a pattern of flowing curves.

The cross-fertilization of ideas and influences, and the variety of
references and effects that enlivens fashion is also revealed in a rather
86 different series of flowing flounced dresses in black organza, very
Spanish in mood; the flounces fall straight and fluid, suggesting some
old-fashioned pre-war flamenco, a mythical Spain like the one that was
to inspire John Galliano in his turn two years later.

Further accidents of drawing: the hand, scarcely lifting from the paper   87
as it traces the motif for a bodice, unintentionally draws a diagonal;
the draughtsman accepts the suggestion: Why not drape the top part?
Alert for signs, or slips, determined to avoid the mechanical, always
ready to seize on the tiniest suggestions that arrive like ethereal
messages, Lacroix is more likely to incorporate than correct any stray
lines that may appear. Since these drawings will also serve as patterns,
and will therefore be subject to interpretation, he sometimes even
gives the same sketch to two of his *premières* so that, having maximized
both the potential for error and the freedom of interpretation, he will
end up with two completely different versions to choose from.

Continuing to ring the changes on the blouse/dress, jacket/coat,
skirt/shorts and reinterpretations of the doublet, he came up with a
bodice with a moiré shirtfront, worn over a meringue-coloured muslin
blouse: a contrast between the stiff material (echoing the body shape)
and the flowing jabots, but here with their positions reversed, the
'structure' encased in a cloud of see-through fabric.

❖

Freddie Mercury represents another of those icons of 'bad' taste so   88
dear to Lacroix, who admired his energy as well as his forceful
rejection of rigid codes of traditional elegance. Although this initial
concept never comes to fruition, we can see how the 'cheap and sexy',
vampy motif of the waistcoat leads on to the cropped blouse/singlet.
In this 'evil genius' collection, as we might well call it, the concept of
the garment that has shrunk is joined by that of the detail that has

been blown up to enormous size (a huge zip, for example). The idea probably came from Lacroix's fascination with doll's clothes. Though their proportions are entirely logical and perfectly reduced in size, they nevertheless usually have to make do with incongruously thick seams, full-size buttons, and so on. Here we have an Alice in Wonderland world, with these bizarre details writ large, so that minor items become invested with hypnotic power. (It is the same problem that faced Martin Margiela when he produced the range of garments that make up the Barbie Doll wardrobe.)

89   The same crazy logic applies to the following sketch, where the lines of force and main seams are accentuated even though they are not in fact 'structural' but purely surface decoration. This is a mischievous trick of reversal, in which the incidental is displayed and the essential concealed. The piping and structural detail are just for show: as Lacroix never ceases to tell us, couture is artifice and make-believe.

⁘

90   Work on the concept continues, also on the narrow colour range of red, white and black, first identified in the photograph of the old Spaniard. Lacroix concerns himself here with combining forms, the whole business of seeing what fits and what does not: '. . . go from large flowers to small,' he notes, 'from small flowers to spots, from spots to lace . . .', as if the prints could change of their own accord. He has always liked lace, with its many associations – *intimo*, as the Italians say, and luxurious. He noticed on a picture of an eighteenth-century

92   costume amazing sashes of black lace that crossed over before tucking

into the bodice and this led to a series of black straps, used to set off or conceal backs or busts, shown in the final parade.

✛

Work in progress, the search for solutions, juggling with different hypotheses: a collection is about experiencing desires and insights – and sometimes about the impossibility of achieving them; there are times when you go down a particular track or try out an idea, which then has to be abandoned. This was the case with the observations on the colour white, mentioned earlier: here we have three more symbols or incarnations of the seventies cast into the final bonfire because the fabric has failed either to adapt to requirements or to live up to expectations: neither piqué (too flat) nor *grain de poudre* (too stiff) were satisfactory. A hypothesis that has been tried and has failed must be discarded. A collection, as it appears afterwards in the press and on the hangers, consists also of the sum of ideas that were rejected because they were impossible or because there was no room for them. Few people even suspect their existence in this world of apparent facility.

98–99

✛

No sooner does one exploration of bad taste have to be thrown out than chance provides another. Just as Lacroix happened across a virtuoso kitsch portrait of Pierre and Gilles (themselves avid worshippers of popular icons) – an image in which the pair appear dressed in Directoire style – he had right in front of him a fabric with a motif identical to that used for the shirt collars in the portrait. It was too good an opportunity, or coincidence, to let slip: he decided to

100–101

make use of these bold prints, with their vague suggestion of psychedelic excess, the airs of a Directoire dandy affected in the incense-burning Carnaby Street era.

❖

102–103 Twiggy was another icon of the age; Lacroix was leafing through a book when he came across a photograph of her in the Ken Russell film *The Boyfriend*. It is an image that seems to draw together all the threads of the collection: the revival of the thirties style in the seventies, the taste for dressing-up and allusion, a girl who paradoxically looks just like a lifesize doll, with the proportions of a child and the old-fashioned sex appeal that goes with lacy beaded fabrics; Lacroix captures its spirit in an experimental sketch that is all 'spun sugar' – myriad strings of tiny beads impossible to distinguish with the naked eye, in cobwebby designs. In a further coincidence, a model friend brought in a 1905 dress which was exactly like the designs in progress.

❖

Once the print has been chosen, together with the model for which it will be used, it has to be laid in position and its final placing determined. As this can only be done full-size, a paper dress is made up and the different patterns are tried out against it and fixed in place. Once the right solution has been found, the actual fabric replaces the mock-up: and the first intimations or ghosts of dresses take shape. The second phase of preparations draws to a close. The first toiles will soon appear, in that definitive and patient process through which each model is brought to perfection.

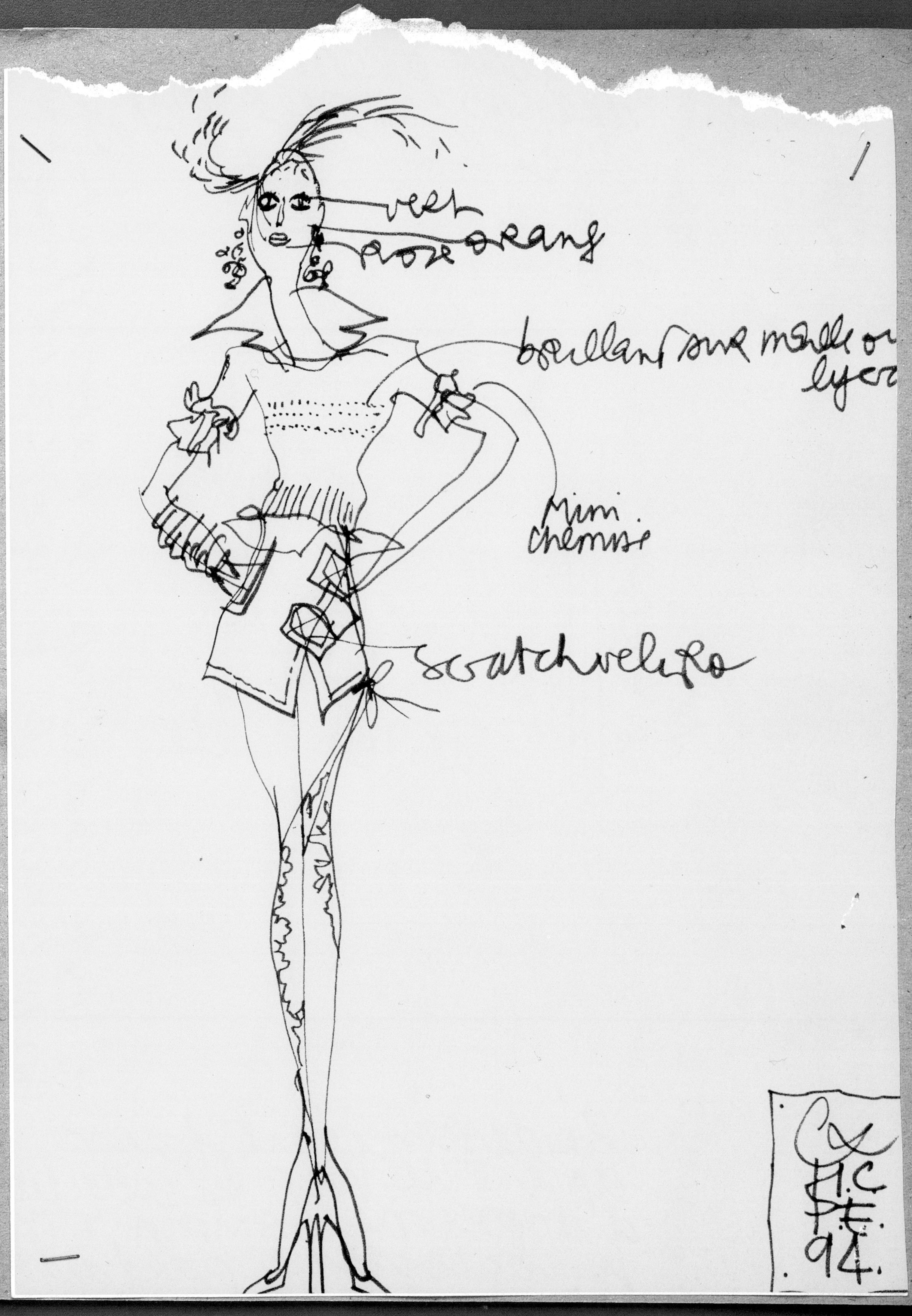

vert
rose orange

brillant sur maille ou
lycra

Mini.
chemise

scratch velcro

H.C
P.E.
94.

les tout premiers vrais
dessins ; jouer sur la
DISPROPORTION

veste
originale

demi
nouveuse

dentelle

devant

+
court

la veste andalouse se rabougrit
se boléro et se blouse/claude se
rallonge en tunique robe sur jupe long?

veste
été

le dessin était fait
avant de voir la collection
d'imprimés GAMMASEIA!
la concordance parfaite
est un bon signe c'j'aime

dessine le même jour
d'imprimés fleuris 1980.

chemise
d'incroyable fleur
en poil body
1930 + laine legere

de tas incroyable

quelle inégales

mouchoir

à mélanger avec tweed 40
les formes XVIIIe en jouant sur
les FAUSSES PROPORTIONS.

je ne sais pas pourquoi   j'ai changé de

toupet →
Menkès

barretts

mini roll

BLAZER
XVIII°
destru
chuel
restru
cturé

← pantalon
de
tennis
1930

← ADIDAS BROGUE XVIII°

← Boots
dentelle noire

BLAZER de tennis 1930 / XVIII°
coiffure pseudo Espagne
Adidas tissu fleuri

ESSAYER DE FA
TRANSPARENT (PLU
DE LA MOUSSELINE

dessiner (trait, face, allure)

chemise
rayée
bleu Blanc
gris →

eche de
brillé

RASTA
COUTURE

envie de vestes de garçonnet
un nouvel esprit masculin
un peu GUY BOURDIN

novembre à début
remembers aussi

QUILT
RIS DS
AVEMENT

mael
dentelle
OL

smo
king
blanc

aiguille

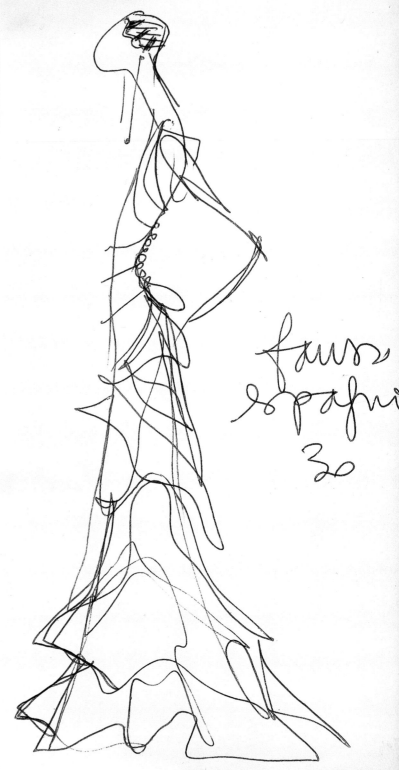

faux
espagn
30

envie de vêtements
tout blancs, de formes
surprenantes un peu
ébériquées et de talons
aiguilles. de maille,
or de collants brodés
et de super plissées

Tout pense de beaucou
plus fluide et faire
se reculer les robes hip
mons vers des robes
de bal avant. guerre
beaucoup de volants
de mousselines

col jabot

blouse LVIII assymetrique

mer et brillant

fond de riens
jupe en dentelle
et crêpe georgette
plisse inégalement

vivre le trait
crayon en
... : la
... = robe.
... = manteau.
... = short
...eaux + fleurs.

Réduire les vestes et le
compliquer beaucoup de
détail historiques imaginaires.
Le blouses devraient pouvoir
être vendues en robe. Jouer
sur les couches transparentes

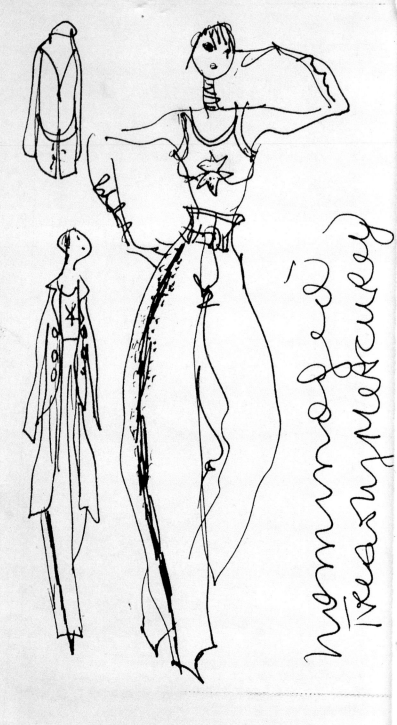

Baroue
Blouse
1900
transparent

hommage à Freddy
Mercury Debardeur
brillant brodé ou noir
ont pantalon un peu
militaire/majorette.

Vêtements 1900
redecquis. (coupés)

veste XVIII essouple

organza plisse

bijou

stretchflur
OU CUIR
SOUPLE

jupettshort

muls

faire apparaitre
les structures qui
n'ont rien à voir
avec la véritable
architecture :
COUTURE = ARTIFICE

ce genre de dessous
devrait être un des
fils conducteurs :
brassières courtes &
clinquante. Shorts
Accessoires Romantiques

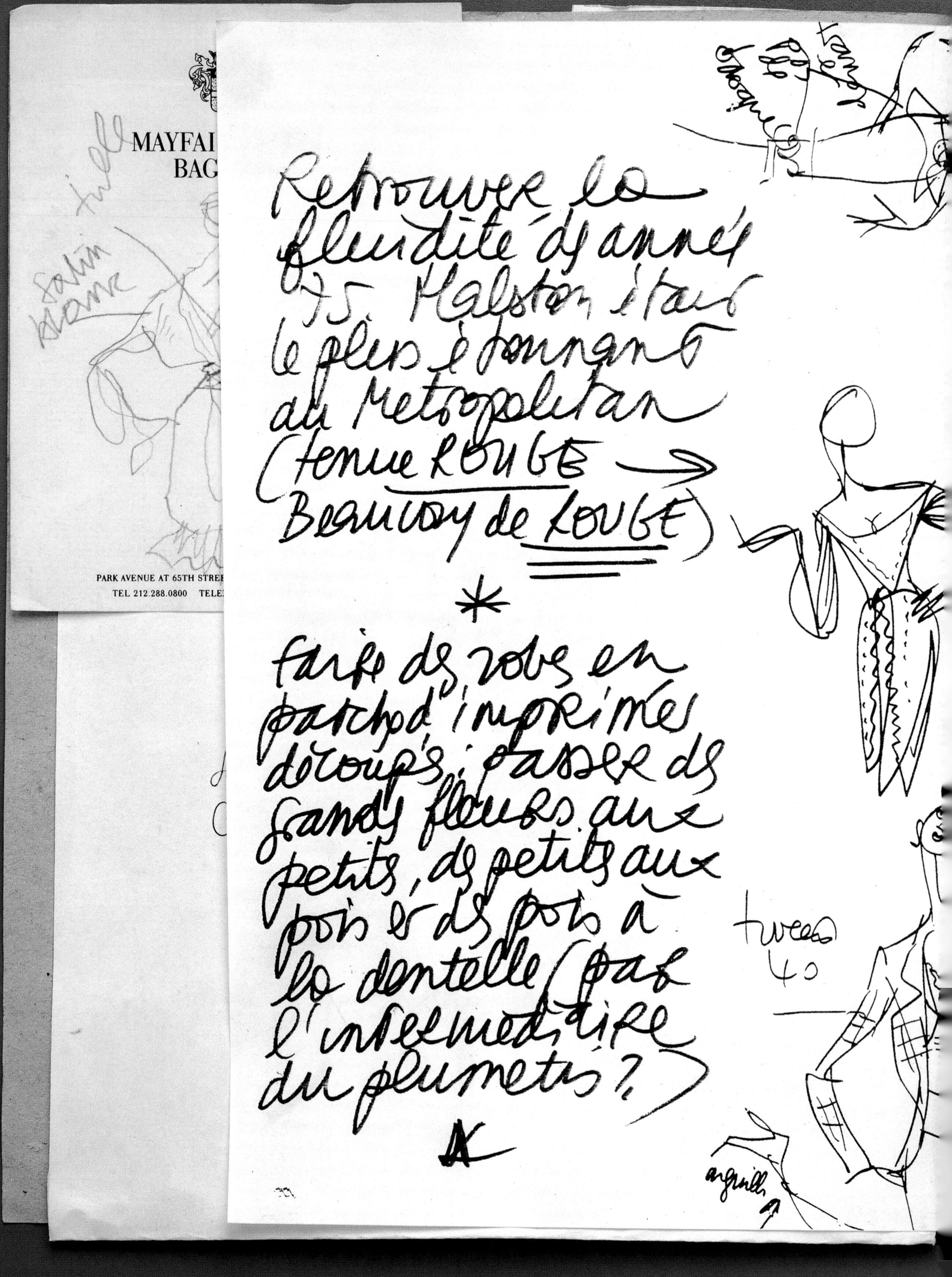

Retrouver la
fleur dité des années
75. Halston était
le plus étonnant
au Metropolitan
(tenue ROUGE →
Beaucoup de ROUGE)

*

faire des robes en
patch d'imprimés
découpés : passer des
grandes fleurs aux
petits, des petits aux
pois et des pois à
la dentelle (pas
l'intermédiaire, dire
du plumetis ?)

tweed
40

MAYFAIR
BAG...

PARK AVENUE AT 65TH STREET
TEL 212.288.0800   TELE...

en volute smokée avec
effet fichu — faire passer
un foulard de dentelle noire

pois + (fleurs?) + dentelle

patch

Cette croix sur un oigne à nefs laissée
pader (cf vste couverture Vogue) faire
faire un shiet sous vste blanche
quelque chose de * Gustave Moreau
er de delacroix : l'hiver la fête le
Baroque er le Sacré pour balancier
les choses les plus élémentaires / Sport

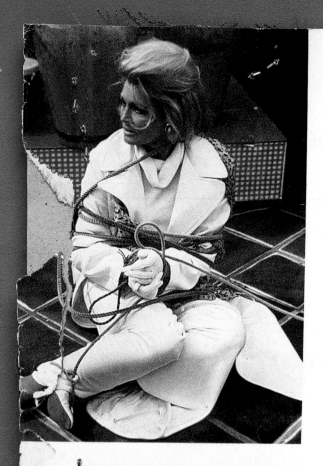

Angie Dickinson
(above) plus Uma
Thurman and friends
in *Even Cowgirls Get
The Blues*

coming attra

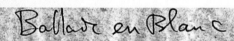

Queer Film Lite – ie gay film tha
directors but continuing desire to
market. First up. Jonathan Demm
with Aids (already a h
but wi'

Hol
b

wann
blunts
Con

c
the
are
th
cons
u

ENVIE DE BLANC

Mas finalement on y arrive : pas d'aucun tissu portable : les transparen y que aux contrée ne sont pas aussi intéressantes, le piqué fait trop prêt-à-porter, le grain de bouche trop masculin. Et moi ? est-ce vrai Wolle je suis trahi par le blanc que je n'aime pas vraimen

Ballade en Blanc

En blanc,
Les Rois du ciel sur terre
Qui parlent d'Amour
En s'interdisant de le faire...
Blanc,
Les chèques du prix de la guerre
Du matériel et des misères...
En blanc,
Les mariages et les chimères,
Les trahisons, les adultères...
Blanc,
Le chat qui méprise les gris,
Les tigrés, les insoumis...
Blanc,
Qui envahit et qui détruit
L'Amérique en quelques nuits...
Blanches,
Les tuniques sévères
Des gardes Blancs de cette terre...
Blanche,
Blanche la mort qui sort
De la bouche du fusil...
Voilà, peut-être pourquoi,
Mon Amour, certains soirs,
Il fait bon d'être un peu noir...
Mon Amour, certains soirs,
Il fait bon d'être un peu noir...

Etienne Rodo-..L..

98

FOR TOM WOL

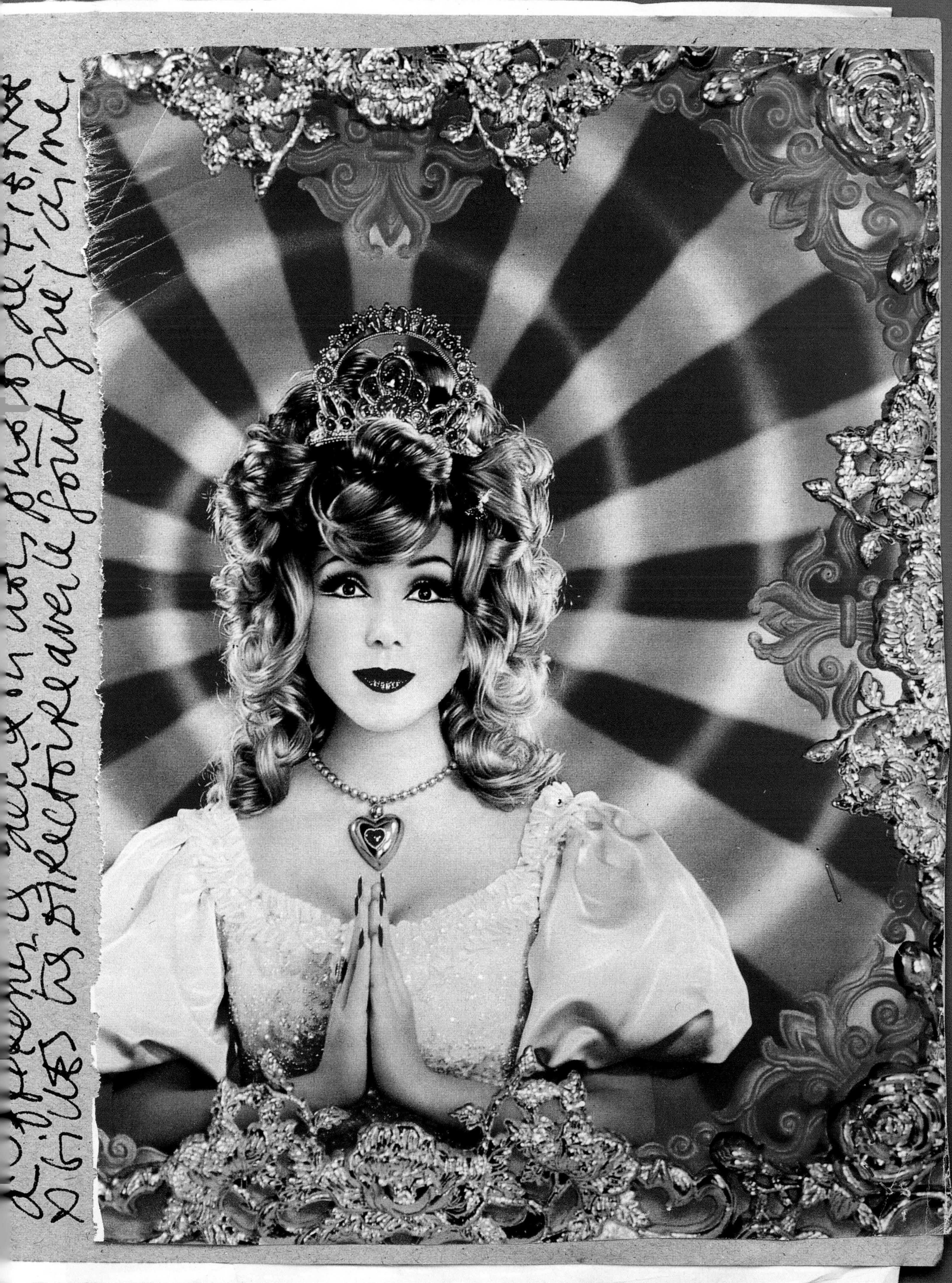
très Directoire avec le fond que j'aime.

volant
petite
fille
tout

Bébés
bouclé

manches

Envie d'un côté très girlish de
poupée Romantique un peu 70.
Les broderies demangage a Lesage
les broderies demanday a Lesage
sont par fautes pour ce thème.

court
ou
LONG
?

on va brouil-
-ler les tissus
trop ancien.
- seulement par
- les fleurs thé
se SAME STREET
de la collection
LANEL brodé
par dessus.
Avec du noir?

nouvea
peintu?
tissu t
formid
qui don
le moti
ci-conti
pour fa
une ju

~3~
The Collection Crystallizes

The organization of a couture house has something in common with a Byzantine theocracy, with its rigid demarcations between head and apprentice seamstresses, between the kingdom of the *flou* – the teams working on lightweight fabrics – and that of the tailors, where the tweeds and heavy fabrics are dealt with. It is to the two head seamstresses of the *flou* that the sketches for this collection will have been passed, now made up as the famous 'toiles': a translation into three dimensions of something that has only existed on paper, the first interpretation of the model, in white or black cloth marked out with ribbon. The toile is then adjusted, fitted and altered, and has samples of various bits of cloth pinned onto it, before being subjected to close scrutiny. Once the relationships of patterns and colours are settled, the next stage can begin, that of cutting out the chosen fabrics and putting all the bits and pieces together.

117   On the first toile, which is inspired by an eighteenth-century Swedish painting, a first variation on the theme of the Rastro jacket appears to be taking shape; the fabric chosen is a red tweed, the intention being to tone down the rather severe, military air of the model.

✛

At this early stage the first hats are also tried out: old straws from Italy, a sort of conical wide-brimmed hat such as might be worn by some mythical Northern European countess on her holidays, the stereotype of a Tsarina in an eighteenth-century tale.

Once collection fever has set in, nothing is immune: there is an avalanche of details and scraps of information that exemplify or add to or confirm the initial inspiration. Coincidences pile up: a detail (fitted coats and tall hats, the Directoire theme) of a late-eighteenth-century painting (object of that short-sighted, partial and some would say purely anecdotal scrutiny in which Lacroix specializes); a picture of a famous gossip columnist, the unconscious reincarnation of a

118–119 *merveilleuse* projected suddenly into a world of glitter and glitz; and,

120 no less bright and flashing in their turn, the sequined samples submitted by Ulrika Liljedahl. And what is it they all add up to? In a word, the chance encounter, on an antique reclining chair, of Madame Récamier and disco.

✛

It is a matter of cutting and pasting, moving things around, matching opposites and reconciling irreconcilables. Modern life – like Lacroix's working methods – is marked by speed, instability, shifts from one thing to the next, going for the obvious 'mix', the quickest fix. It is also marked by the ease of using photocopies and stencils to change or transpose things *ad infinitum*, always with a different definition, a different grain, a new reality for images and motifs.

That is why the highest quality calf leather, of the most extra-ordinary suppleness, softness and delicacy, will be subjected to the most prosaic of procedures, having illustrations and photos copied onto it (gaining in evocative power what they lose in clarity and precision). The Beatles and the young *novillero* Swan Soto are to make their appearance later, the first image is the face of a famous model; virginal, in Lacroix's eyes, and referring back to the Lesage Virgin Mary and the primitive splendours of the ex-voto piece, it is translated here by modern methods of reproduction into a blurred hieratical symbol. 122

A further coincidence – the day's post brings with it this flower photograph by Don Freeman, its inky, washed-out, faded tones echoing the deep, muted, iridescent purple of the calf leather; it happens also to chime in with Lacroix's ideas on the new range of colours he is beginning to develop for future collections. 123

⁜

The preparation of a collection is a matter of competing and conflicting priorities, always at the mercy of delays and complications 124–125

in production, whether or not the materials can be made to work and the desired effects achieved. Straw 'cartwheels' on the one hand, embossed leather on the other – these were the options available for bags and accessories. Lacroix had originally thought of actual wickerwork baskets in the shape of straw hats, which would provide a contrast with the rich taffetas and embroidery; but that proved technically a non-starter, and in the end metal strips covered with gold taffeta were woven together to give the effect of recalcitrant wickerwork. These unique objects were made by virtuoso craftsmen working for the feather-dresser Lemarié. In the end embossed leather won out. This, with all its historical connotations, richness of texture, colour and surface interest, was to be the material used for many of the designs that appear on these pages.

⁜

126–127 Two preliminary try-outs. The shot taffeta arrives and is immediately draped over a wooden mannequin to get the full effect: Lacroix decides to dress it up still further by asking Lesage to add embroidery. To counterbalance that richness, the rest of the outfit needs to be kept simple – a satin shift or gold Lycra vest. The arrival of materials which have been ordered and expected, but then forgotten, always creates a tremor which upsets plans and preconceived ideas – Lacroix is scrupulous in noting its effects.

Elsewhere, a toile is being adapted to make an idea work and transform a theme into a reality. The link has already been made between the patchwork lining of a Provençal jacket and the motorcyclist's jacket with its constellation of emblems and motifs. Experiment has made it clear that colour ranges will have to be restricted, so it is more a matter of combining materials (wool and taffeta). Several bits of fabric are pinned onto the toile to decide the position of the different pieces and the relationship between them. There is also a further development in Lesage's embroidery of the Virgin Mary, the bodice of which it had been decided to reverse; a fitting takes place of one of those historic corsets that Madame Boutard manages to come up with every season.   **127** (A specialist in corsetry and a theatrical costumier, it was through her work that she first met Lacroix, at a play.) Once the design, model and technique have been fixed, it is finally decided to make it up in furnishing fabric, echoing the look of the Virgin Mary print.

❖

Deliveries of Calais lace are timed to coincide with collections and   **128–129** seasons. Some pieces are selected for their designs and the quality of their filigree, and these form part of the little treasure trove of materials available for a collection, which Lacroix loves to come and look at in the early morning before the arrival of his head seamstresses. He tries to plan the work in advance, and organize the shape of the day. This is his way of encouraging, or of simply allowing to happen, those lucky matches, apparent coincidences or happy accidents which matter so much to him.

❖

Now comes a crucial moment for the collection, and for that mysterious process called fashion, when the look that will be seen in the streets is finally decided. In December 1993, fashion was still wringing its hands in atonement for excesses, real or imagined. The mood was for restraint and suffering, for spurning ostentation and embracing simplicity: fashion for a time of crisis, when people decided not to display any visible sign of wealth (since this would be seen as offensive), giving propriety as an excuse. Even Lacroix's fashion (a theatrical parody of ostentation) did not escape being the butt of what were on the whole rather stupid attacks in some of the more puritanical papers.

129, 130   To put behind him something that had become an inconvenient symbol, making an obligatory appearance at every show since he had reinvented it – namely, the pouf – Lacroix had for several seasons taken the decision to omit it altogether from his collections. Yet in this season he decided to present a 1987-style pouf dress, complete with the spots that used to be such an important feature of his designs for Patou (a motif that has cropped up here already).

Lacroix could foresee even then the need for a change of key, the return to glamour and sophistication, historical effects, collages and parodies, something the rest of us would not fully appreciate until two years later, as designers branched out in the new directions characteristic of today's fashion.

✢

THE COLLECTION CRYSTALLIZES

A dialogue is set up between the drawings – *ad hoc* variations, preparatory sketches done in a vacuum – and the possibilities suggested by the suppliers' wares: lace by Forster Willi in particular; the figured flounces, elaborate tucks, ruching and goffering created by the embroiderers; and the rippling surfaces of the feather-dressers. Little black dresses in subtle textures are the result, a sort of cross between the bohemian chic of Biba in 1970 and the vampy appeal of disco.

⁘

In an abrupt change of key, the idea of a white bride surfaces – it   132–133
would be a first in Lacroix's collections. All the available items in that
non-colour are to be pressed into service, supplemented by repeat
orders from Forster Willi. The dress for the show will consist of a
basque top in piqué and a full skirt in piqué and embroidered
organdie. The only irreverent touch in an otherwise too decorous
ensemble would be the headgear (a cap?).

⁘

As well as the essentials of a collection, other things have   134–135
to be considered as well – things that from an outsider's point of
view might wrongly be considered as incidental: the set, for
example, the decor, the announcements, and the images used to
accompany or advertise the show. There is the decoration of the
stage, which sets the tone for the invited guests, and the design of
the invitation card. At least a month before the occasion, these must
be settled and the broad outlines of the design finalized. Lacroix has
decided to abandon his usual plant theme in favour of a painted

backcloth – allusive, luxuriant and lighthearted, in the manner of Christian Bérard or Oliver Messel, he explains – that suggests the forties, and an exuberant theatricality. The invitation card, newly designed each season, is accompanied by a poem written by Françoise Lacroix; it too bears appropriate symbols: a forties hairstyle tied back in a net, and a very structured fitted basque jacket reminiscent of the eighteenth century – a choice of symbols that is also nerve-wracking since it has to be arrived at when the overall ensemble is still evolving, or at least lacks many of its aspects: nevertheless, a firm commitment has to be made.

❖

138–139 Some of the original starting-points or inspirations re-surface in new incarnations, at a further stage of their evolution. The Rastro jacket, it is decided, needs its too obviously Spanish appearance softened (or countered?) by the use of a pareu. Danielle Boutard has recreated the approximate shape of the 1880 jersey top seen at the Metropolitan Museum; now the toile must be covered in the cut-out photocopies of flowers that serve as models for the embroideries.

As the to-and-fro begins of toiles awaiting readjustment and finished models, a dress descends the stairs in its almost final form – the clearest possible statement of the Directoire theme. Lacroix suggests using machine-stitched pleats to make the ensemble look less 140–141 of a period piece. On a waiting toile, a bolero is used that is based on a famous picture of an Arlesienne; it will finally be made up in a dark fabric with a leafy design, one shoulder bearing an embroidery based on one of the primitive holy images considered at the very start of the collection.

✣

A narrow little top, long loose pyjamas, flowing fabric: all so character-istic of the forties, and devastatingly elegant, as an old photo shows. Various notes on the fabrics that it will be made up in: parasol stripes; patterns like those found on old-fashioned chintz curtains; a Provençal print, an abstract pattern that suffered an accident in manufacture – one seized on eagerly and retained by Lacroix, who asked for the colours to blur together and fade into each other in the final stage of printing.   142–143

A different range has arrived, which includes some large flower motifs, handprinted in the bold colours of comics or cartoons; but the print provides no more than a starting point, it is merely one element in the game of screens and layers in which Lacroix's work consists: traced, cut out and laid over another tracing, it is finally sent to the embroiderer for one last operation.   144–145

✣

At the same time, work goes ahead on choosing the accessories, whether feathers, metal or embossed leather. This still somewhat incomplete jumble of items will form the basis of a sort of magic chest, the idea being that you should be able to rummage through it, usually at the very last moment, the evening before the show, as the outfits are being put together. It thus offers a small repertoire of possibilities, tiny details waiting to slot into place, motifs that   146–147 tie in with this or that hypothesis (whether verifiable or not). Chance plays another trick: a shawl pops up just as someone is thinking about using small umbrellas and makes a Spanish-style fringed parasol.

152–153   Three weeks before the show, the pace hots up. The first photos have to be taken for previews in specialist magazines. As well as accessories and the set for the show, this also means that the hairstyles have to be chosen. The first efforts by Daniel Frenna, who has worked with Lacroix since 1982, are based on the Récamier style, but they are finally abandoned in favour of hairnets and chignons. A further constraint is that the hairstyles must tie in with the line of the hats (now beginning to arrive: forties-style boaters). The ground rules of the collection may already have been laid down, but it is not until the night before the show that, item by item, and model by model, this or that hairstyle or hat will be chosen.

It is that typical Lacroix obsession that things should not become fixed – restricting possibilities, opportunities for cross-fertilization, interesting combinations, suggestions of new avenues to explore – that leads him to consider a radical new idea for the hats: abstract motifs by

157   Matisse and Picasso, astonishing asymmetrical creations that will set off the collection's 'forties' line. In practice the contrast is too extreme and the idea lapses.

                        ❖

154   Trials, proposals, modifications and permutations: the Polaroid of a finished dress is coloured, embellished and accessorized; a lavish

arrangement of feathers is suggested, which would completely alter the silhouette, but it is not used. Work with Lesage continues, and he is asked to make a bodice with a metallic-looking skirt of overlapping scallops covered in iridescent lace, fastened with an imitation jewel . . . A virtuoso embroidery of a bird, ordered   159 previously, is tried out against the striped taffeta on which it will eventually be used (and which contains exactly the same colours as the original dress, which only comes to light later). The match is perfect.

⊹

The face of Christy Turlington was to have been used for the   162–163 reproductions of the image of the Madonna. When she was prevented from coming, the substitute eventually decided on was André-Charles Beau's icon of the *novillero* Swan Soto, with its hieratic sensuality, its echoes of a quasi-religious experience, that tragic ceremonial that lies at the very heart of Lacroix's culture. This image too was to undergo a whole series of changes.

As the fittings come thick and fast, as the bridal gown appears in its final form, topped by its cap, as embroideries and motifs are juggled, serious thought is given to the final elements of the jigsaw, throwing out anything that does not work, choosing tights and bodies. The show is now only a week away; the dresses have taken on their final form; they are grouped in sequences, themes or clusters, and they need backing, emphasis, reorganization; every evening of this last week Lacroix uses for fine-tuning the delicate mechanism and supplying the final touches, those apparently insignificant elements of the complex staging of a collection, where absolutely nothing is left to chance; the musical accompaniments that echo the rhythms of the parade give the models a beat to follow and encourage them to express themselves: these are all done in association with Laurent Godard.

Now the final hours of feverish activity have arrived, with the race to make that last alteration, with the obligatory sleepless nights, the hustle and bustle. The preparations are completed; time for a new ritual to begin, bringing with it a whole new set of problems.

At nine o'clock on the morning of Sunday 16 January 1994, the first models appear on the catwalk.

100% FIL
E

premier essayage rassurant
et dynamisant. tweed + ganse
de taffetas + dentelle sur un
pantalon d'homme et un
pull à faire tricoter chez hein.

19
XII
93.

nouvelle
Madame
Récamier
dans le style
commencé

in

te

?

?

t

Suzy at home

118

rencontre hasardeuse des échantillons
de sequins or d'Ulrika avec un pull
de soie → dessous pour une veste juste
trop 1890 ce qu'il faut de Mme Janine.
finalement maille & paillettes sont
un peu oxbrematifs ; on mettra un
top en argent + une peste fleurs or

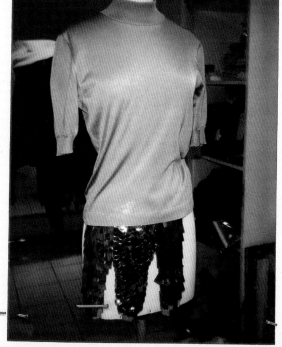

On peut tout imprimer ou transferer
sur le cuir des gants et cheri, ty sur
les tshirts de plus en plus divine Madou
Mais elle ne sera finalement pas a Paris.

DON FREEMAN
Les Pivoines, 1993. Blue Print, 91X104 cm

Ls plus beaux taffetas changeant de la
saison. Ne pas hesiter à ls rebroder chez
Lesage à condition d avoir une chemise
de nuit en satin et un maillot or desso

*

Dur de choisir ls patches, de me larges
taffetas et lainage + ruchs tricolores

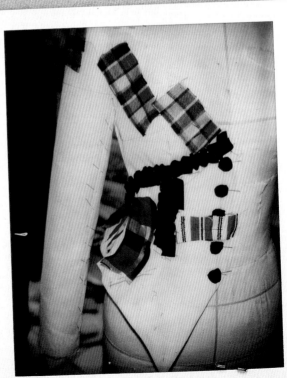

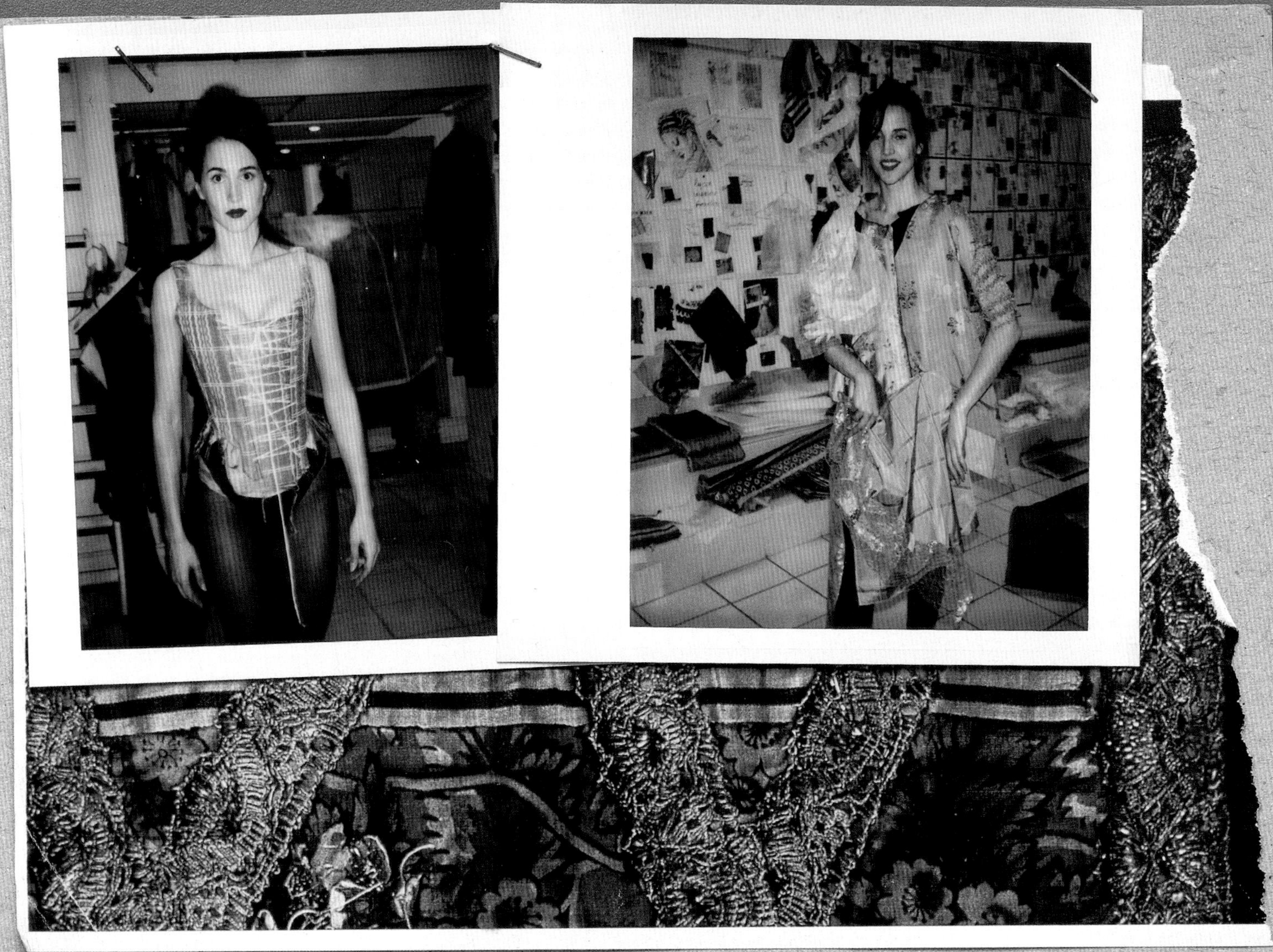

la mariée sera finalement paysanne
remplacer le tulle initial par une overdose
de dentelle, brocart et satin brodé XVIIIe

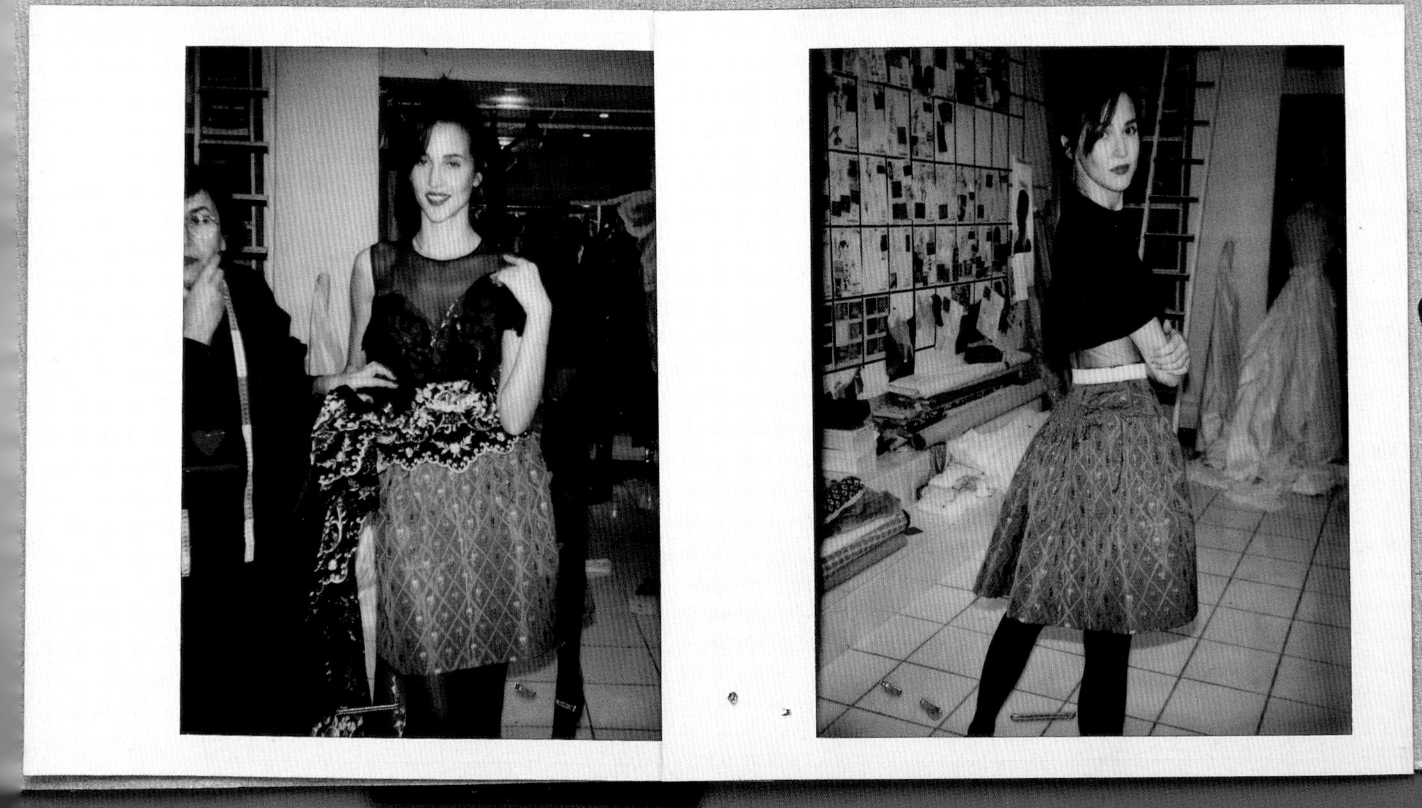

Gschada Goya

KUNGLIGT
KLÄDD
KUNGLIGT
MODE

22 ou 23/ on a trouvé les bons motifs de
XII/93 guile de dentelle pour réaliser
le plastron ancienne 1900

Retour aux noy 80.
Commerche. Il sou
tien forge de dus,
sous deviendra
une rose de dentel.
le à part. Retour
au pont 87 aussi

LEMARIE
H.C P/E 94

De même que pour le tournesol, elle a rendu
en vrai robe de mariée. C'est presque une
B. cape d'échanté. Dommage de rester

24 fév

casquette?

Mais il faudra lui trouver un moyen d'avoir
l'allure du reste de la collection, car lo collerate
une femme sur moto - Pourquoi pas une casquette?

24 Décembre 93.
Jean-Jacques a eu l'idée
de faire un décor plus
base que végétal, cette
année à l'Inter-Conti-
-rental - votre livre
Bérard + O. Messel -
demandée à Michael
de la faille Japonaise
comme sur le tableaux

Dimanche dernier.
Françoise a écrit
le poème pour la
carte d'invitation
qui est imprimée.

Carreaux sur des fleurs durables,
Rayures à jamais osées,
Merveilleuse autant qu'incroyable,
Fervente avec un cœur doré,
Gymnaste alerte et désirable,
C'est l'asphalte qui la fait planer.

F.L.

LAST SEASON OR
PAST DAYS RESULTS
OR INDICATIONS
CAN'T BECAME
ANY RULE OR
LAW FOR THE
NEXT SEASON
BEHAVIOURS

-3 ou 24/XII/93 .

Veste réussie. A
broder? ox on ou
reussi a donner
l'impression que la
taille se ne pas dans
le tissage. Bas?
ni...portefeuille VELCRO

un ds dernier modes
à décider. Se tissus
sont ne ensembles
L paillette d'abord
annulés ils ont rejoint
la dentelle & clusive
oubliée aussi. Sades
l'idée de la broderie?

137

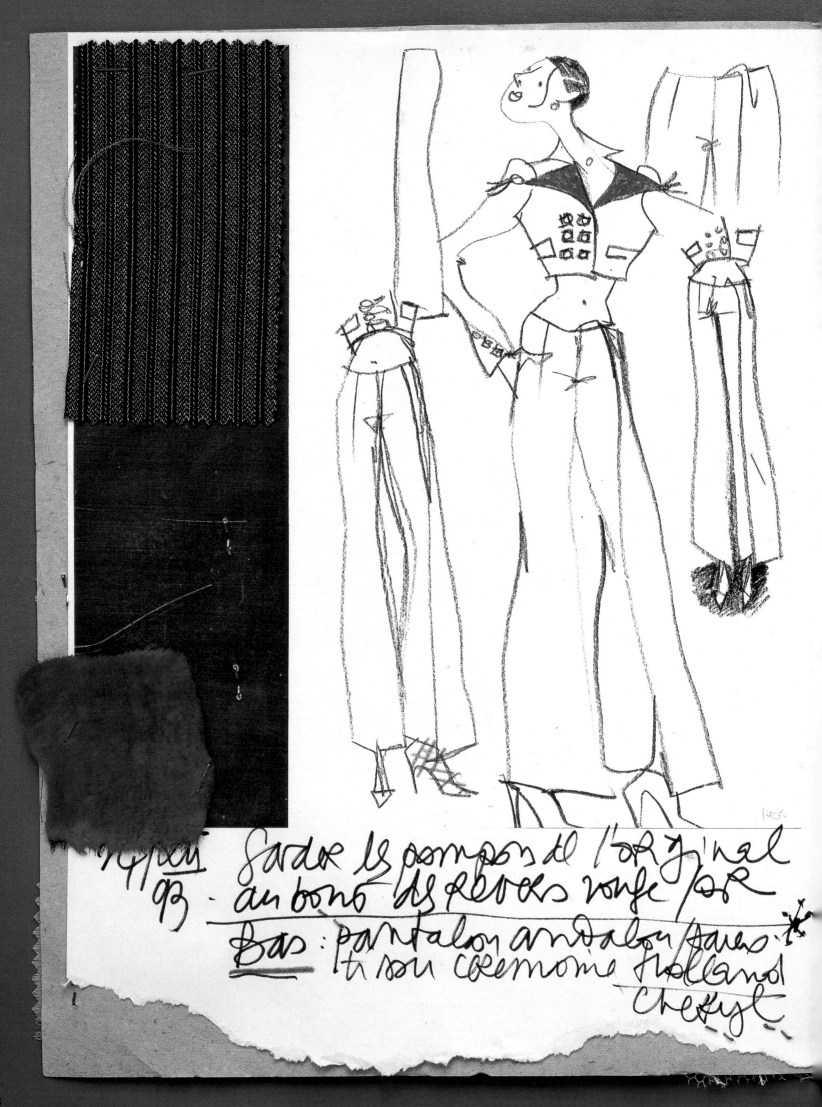

JEUDI 23

A LIBERTÉ DES AUTRES ÉTEND A MIENNE A L'INFINI - BAKOUNINE

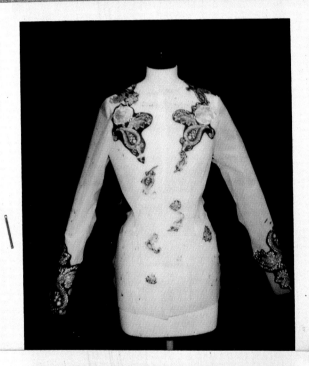

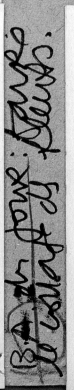

Spare le fleurs
"chimère" pour
la belle air le cor
— en 1880 de Famele

Bakounine pour : Faire
l'instant et fleurs.

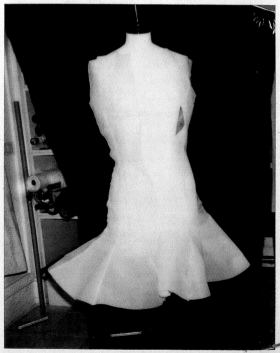

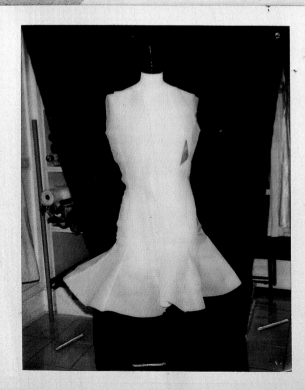

m Anton
in dress!
Broderie
Menendez
Brothers!

[Handwritten journal notes in French, largely illegible cursive:]

spring 40.
... reintroferait
... palement
2 shirt dire(...)
aujourd'hui les
... mons mouvn
... als oui le
même fente
... pyiama (x)
... un haut
fleurs fabri.
toujours le mini
... ill directrice
... ulerika-la
... inxieme robe
... revue dans ce
... aprés "liberatio
... fait remplacée
par un second
... overlay uni
... l'esprit
... Rouge. les,
... per forme
... trouver la
... sur couleur
... supplemen-
taire. —

143

de patch-work "CARTOON" for Vanity Fair "

Jupe de tennis
— blanc — ou jupe
de cuir argent ou
platine matelassée?
Body lycra métal
de toutes façons.

29/XII
93.   Sac en marabout et autruche frisée

Sac en plumes

châle

Bambou

Lumen

châle

Bambou

Lumen

ombrelle en châle espagnol ; manche bambou + lumen
(Santos de Rarailles)

146

30/XII
93

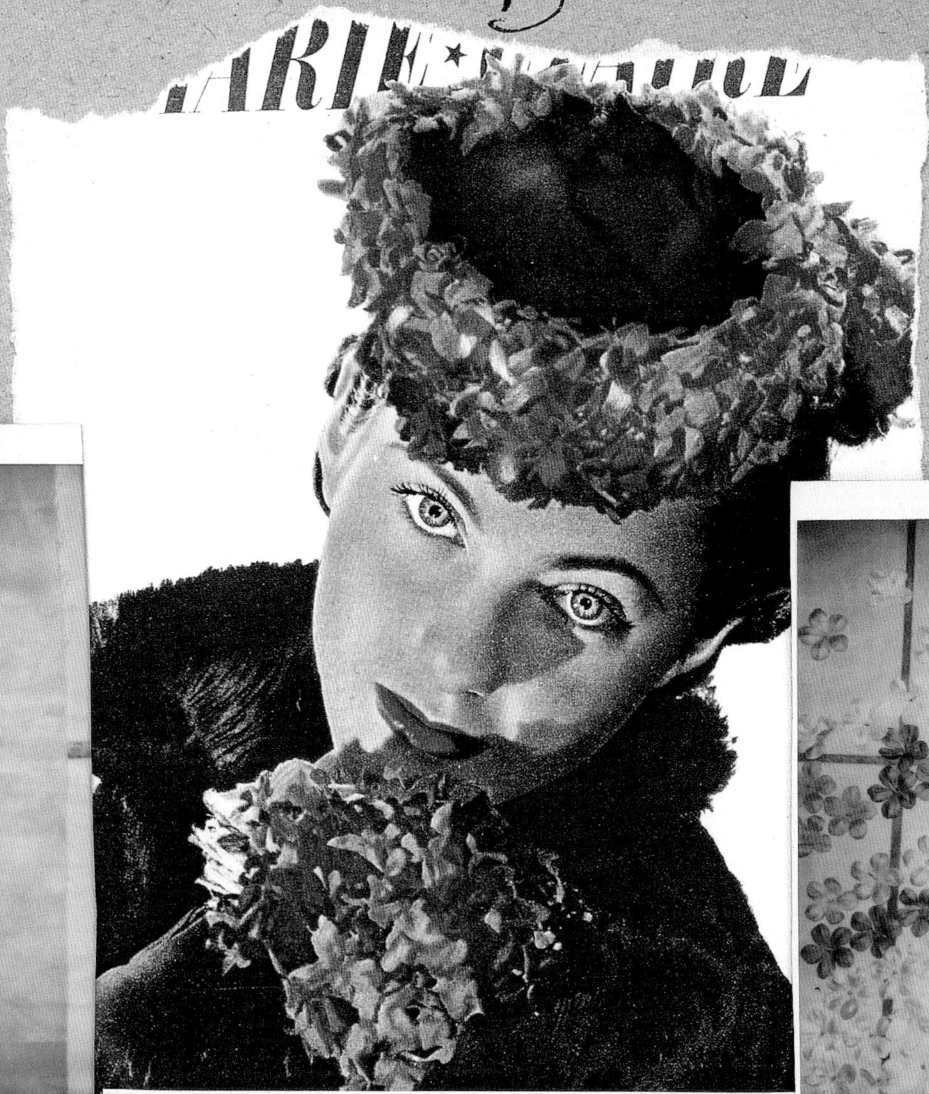

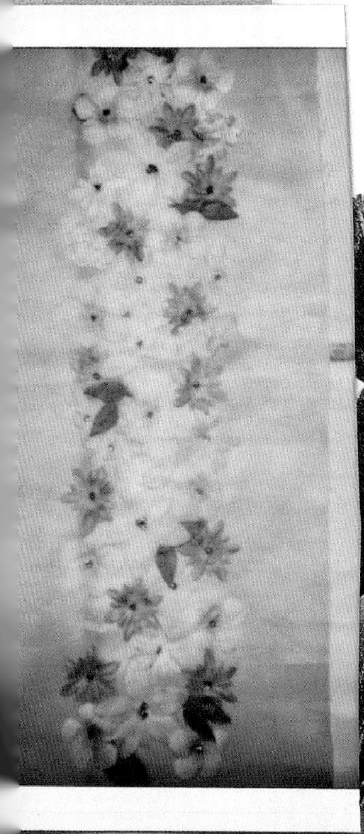

travailler avec Lesage

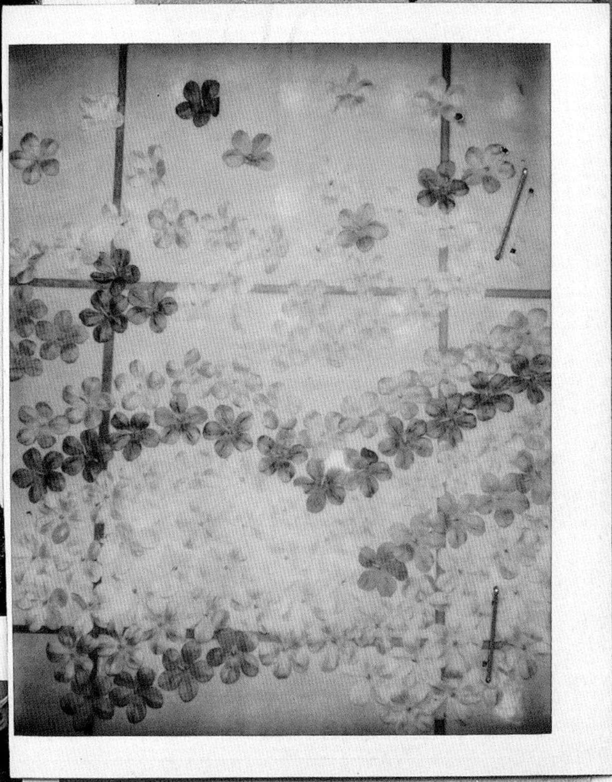

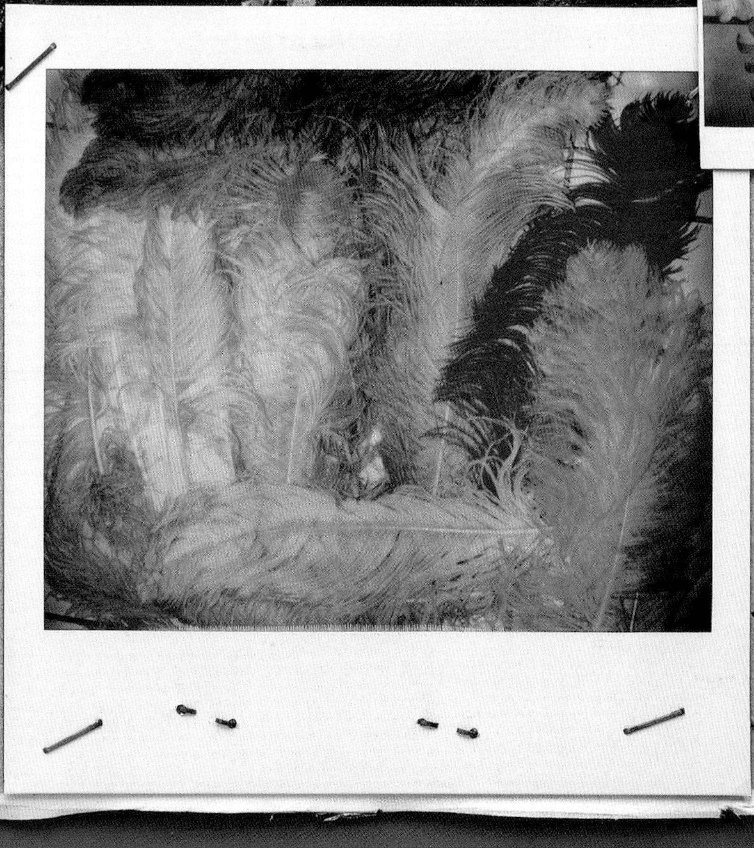

Collage pour les gants

collage pour les gants

31/XII
93

DONNER LES DERNIERS CROQUIS

Dernière matinée de l'année;
Ultime hommage (vem après) à
Louise de Vilmorin et ses grands
pulls 1948, e Vog et blouses victoriennes

Dernière évidence:
la dentelle oubliée
de Jacob Schlaepfer
mordorée si parfaite
pour la mariée (suite)

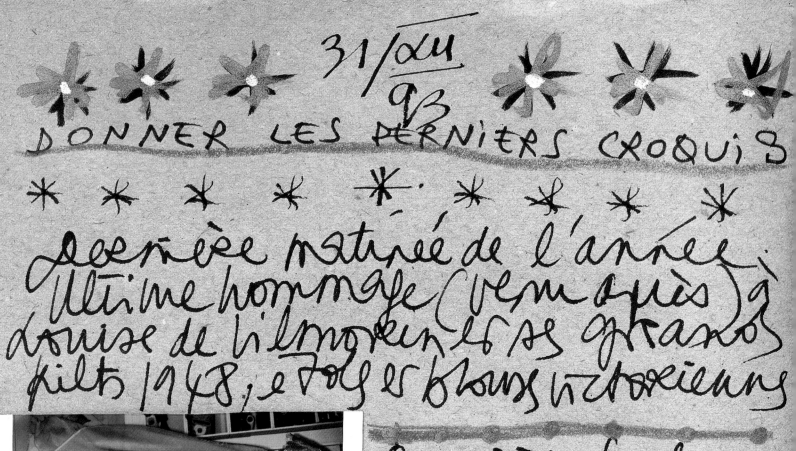

La dame
de Verrières avait
fait de son salon
bleu un asile
pour poètes,
écrivains ou
cinéastes de génie.

151

Suzanne le regarde Suzanne se regarde Suzanne

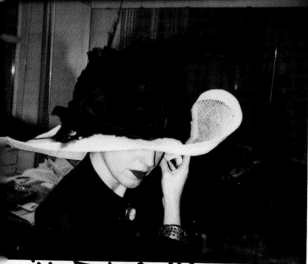

153

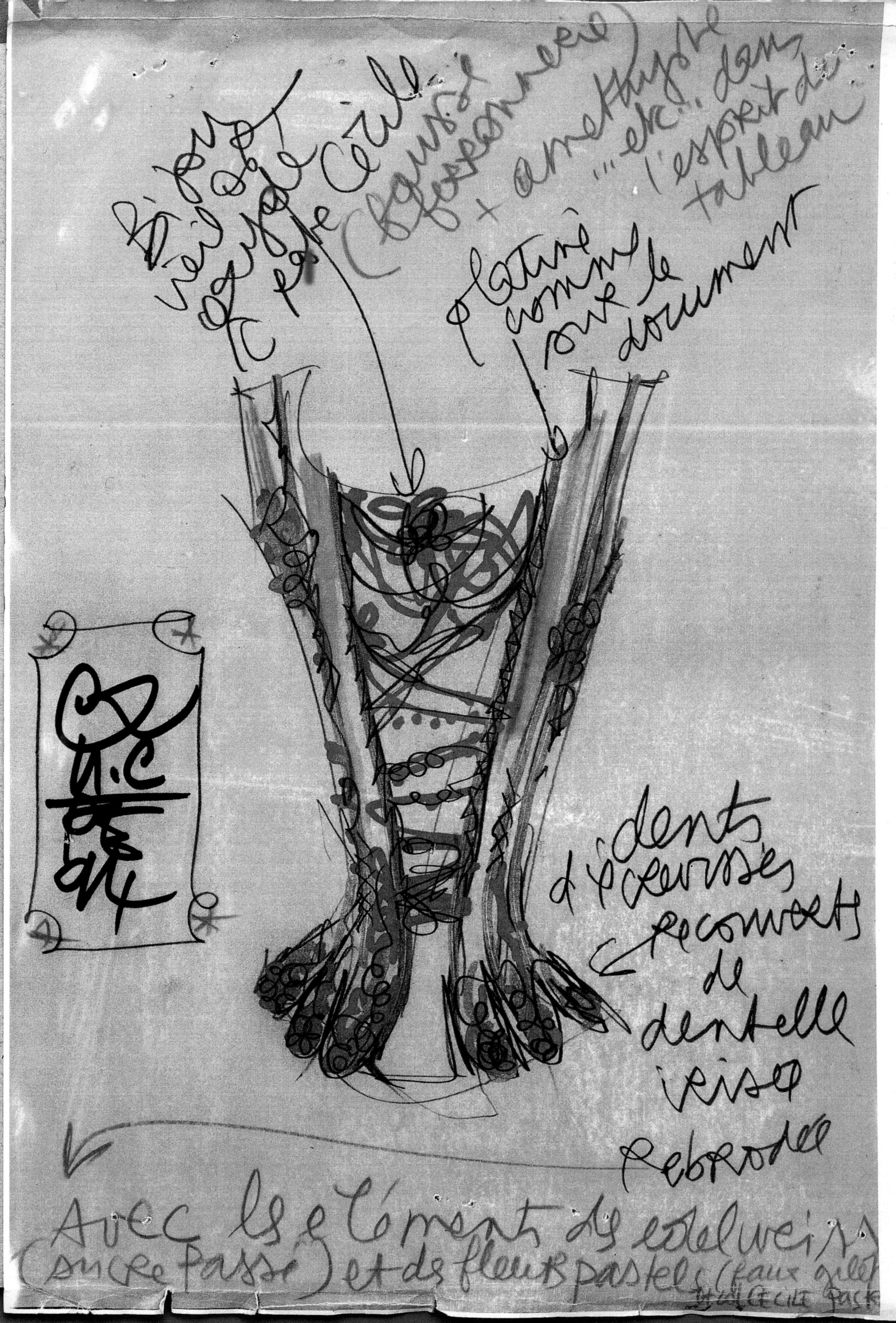
+ améthyste ... etc... dans l'esprit du tableau
platine comme sur le document
dents d'écrevisses recouverts de dentelle irisée rebrodée
Avec les éléments des edelweiss (sucre passé) et des fleurs pastels (faux gilet)

Vogue

ASCOT FASHIO
MA 1939 1
PRICE ONE SHI

FV 1939 Bouché. Suzy

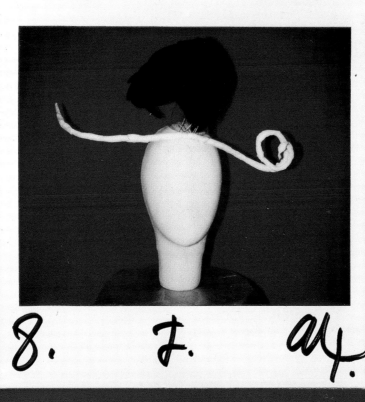

8. 7. 94.

Quelque chose de
la Cendrillon de
Walt Disney avec
les guirlandes ...

diminues le top
ajoutes fleurs↑
trelessienne 40
l'on tire les Rois →

Le jupe de Kirtsch
est réussie, Raffin-
ée, marque de feui-
lle dans le dos mais
en gros. La robe
anche de mariée
en crêône avec les
asquette, et le corse
u chinois M & OK.

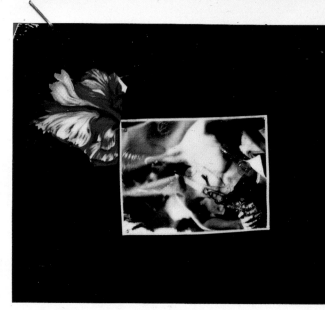

TOUTES LES ERREURS
OU IMPERFECTIONS
DU JOUR (TROP DE
..., PAS ASSEZ DE
... ... &C ...) DOIVENT
ETRE INTERPRETES
COMME DES SIGNES
DES DIEUX ET ERE
GARDES TELS QUE
JUSQU'A LA FIN

167

Essais de fleurs noires sur le
paille patinées chez ORCO.

PROBLÈME DES BÉRETS

Les poches de cuir verni de S.B
fonctionnent avec le tweed ms
il faut   changer
le chêne   voir shoot

LA Problè.   me de
body roy   la veste
brodé Jau.   ne. On
remplace   ne par
dela den.   telle avec
problème   de tubar
                                   aussi

168

naturels ?

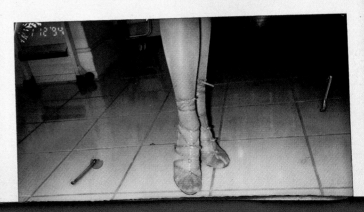

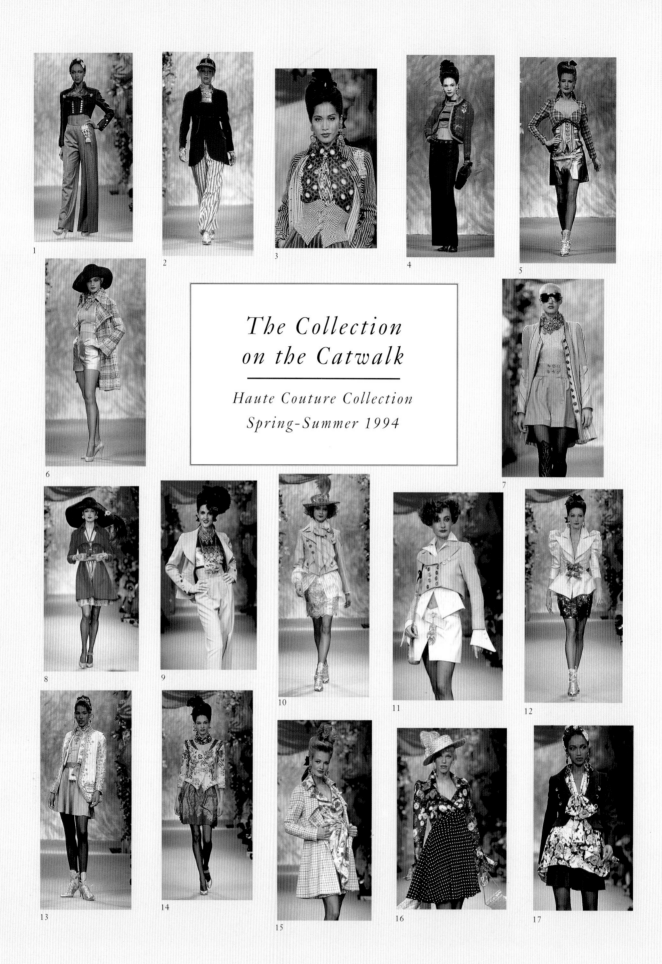

The Collection
on the Catwalk

Haute Couture Collection
Spring-Summer 1994

18

19

20

21

22

23

24

25

26

27

28

29

30

31

32

33

34

35

36

37

38

39

40

41

42

43

44

45

46

47

48

49

50

51

Programme of the Collection

CHRISTIAN LACROIX
HAUTE COUTURE COLLECTION
SPRING–SUMMER 1994

ONE
Black wool bolero with dupion sleeves and gold stamped 'blood-red' velvet collar. Black threaded grey wool wrap-over pants.
MODEL: KATOUCHA

TWO
Satin trimmed and knotted navy crêpe kick-pleat jacket. Gold top. Wide navy and white striped pants.
MODEL: EMMA SJÖBERG

THREE
White threaded chocolate crêpe peplum jacket. Black, white and red spotted shirt. Wide pants with matching 'vest-belt'.
MODEL: ANNA BAYLE

FOUR
Black lace and taffeta bolero trimmed with red tweed. Short sailor sweater. Red threaded navy pants with buttoned yoke.
MODEL: JULIA SCHÖNBERG

FIVE
Ruching-trimmed red, white and blue striped check taffeta and wool patchwork waistcoat jacket. 'Pewter' leather wrap-over skirt.
MODEL: KAREN MULDER

SIX
Handwoven pastel and grey frock-cardigan. Iridescent 'tortoiseshell' sequinned T-shirt. 'Champagne' leather shorts.
MODEL: AMBER VALLETTA

SEVEN
Pastel and mustard handwoven candy-striped silk frock-coat. Antique gold top. Honey men's fabric 'Directoire style' shorts.
MODEL: EVE SALVAIL

EIGHT
'Tomato' crêpe tunic-coat. Short 'coffee and milk' striped chiffon dress with flower-embroidered hem.
MODEL: VICTORIA HERNANDO

NINE
'Sand' grain de poudre men's style suit. Velvet and black chiffon 'cross' T-shirt.
MODEL: SUZANNE VON ACHINGER

TEN
Salmon striped cotton spencer. Chiffon shirt with 'oatmeal' linen dickey. Pink lace covered sequinned chiffon skirt.
MODEL: SHALOM HARLOW

ELEVEN
Short straw-embroidered flaxen silk linen jacket. Beige chiffon shirt with moiré dickey. Matching whipcord skirt.
MODEL: FLORENCE VENTURI

TWELVE
Jacket with 'meringue' silk and 'praline' bowed puff sleeves. Gold embroidered lamé organza modesty. Gold sequinned skirt.
MODEL: CARLA BRUNI

THIRTEEN
Embroidered sand moiré and sky-blue satin 18th-century double torero jacket with raw silk back. Oatmeal silk sweater. Short men's-look woollen skirt.
MODEL: SONIA COLE

FOURTEEN
Provençal flower-embroidered 'sunflower' satin caraco-jacket. 'Paisley' scarf printed silk skirt.
MODEL: JULIA SCHÖNBERG

FIFTEEN
Short pale yellow check tweed coat. Flower-printed 'jade' silk tunic. Bright yellow check taffeta mini-kilt.
MODEL: KAREN MULDER

SIXTEEN
Long 'straw' check tweed cardigan. Trompe-l'oeil dress with high-draped flowered black organza blouse and black and white polka dot crêpe skirt.
MODEL: EMMA SJÖBERG

SEVENTEEN
Red threaded black men's fabric spencer-bolero. Multicolour bouquet printed black silk blouse dress. Matching shorts.
MODEL: KATOUCHA

EIGHTEEN
Bronze and claret knit knotted bolero. 'Herbal' printed red silk T-shirt. Garance and saffron tone-on-tone Provençal design pyjama pants belted with matching striped draping.
MODEL: ANNA BAYLE

NINETEEN
Dress with white, red and black spotted smocked 'shawl' neckline over lace-incrusted spotted crêpe romper-dress.
MODEL: CARLA BRUNI

TWENTY
Multicolour flower patchwork embroidered lace and organza dress.
MODEL: SHALOM HARLOW

TWENTY-ONE
Crêpe caraco-jacket with black red and green, floral organza skirt over tiny red-flowered black crêpe romper-dress.
MODEL: FLORENCE VENTURI

TWENTY-TWO
Poppy printed black crêpe dress with scooped-shoulder straps over embroidered red organza jumpsuit.
MODEL: AMBER VALLETTA

TWENTY-THREE
Short meadow-flowers-scattered blue chiffon dress with draped neckline and shoulder straps over roses-embroidered organza petticoat.
MODEL: EVE SALVAIL

TWENTY-FOUR
Black tulle bolero and
red and gold silk top
with black lace
appliqués.
18th-century short blue
silk skirt with flower-
embroidered girdle belt.
MODEL: SUZANNE VON
ACHINGER

TWENTY-FIVE
Short black and beige
polka-dot silk dress
with one shoulder strap
tucked up over ruffled
black tulle petticoat.
MODEL: VICTORIA
HERNANDO

TWENTY-SIX
Black and white polka-
dot faille pouf jacket
with 'oatmeal' guipure
appliqué.
Black lace and piqué
bra-dress with 'oatmeal'
lace hem.
MODEL: SONIA COLE

TWENTY-SEVEN
Long black crêpe
cardigan-jacket.
Long black satin top
with embroidered
reproduction of portrait
of Swan Soto by
Alain-Charles Beau.
Eggshell satin shorts.
MODEL: KATOUCHA

TWENTY-EIGHT
Navy wool mini-jacket.
'Egg-white' satin
chiffon shirt with moiré
dickey. Antique gold
embroidered lace and
chiffon skirt-petticoat.
MODEL: EMMA SJÖBERG

TWENTY-NINE
Pearl and gold
embroidered navy silk
jersey girdle-cardigan
over white chiffon
'tennis' skirt.
MODEL: KAREN MULDER

THIRTY
Bouquet embroidered
black and écru cloqué
organza top. 18th-
century gold threaded
grey silk 'tennis skirt-
shorts' with
buttoned yoke.
MODEL: EVE SALVAIL

THIRTY-ONE
Lace-incrusted écru
tulle kimono knotted
with a candy-striped
taffeta belt over satin
romper-dress with
guipure yoking.
MODEL: ANNA BAYLE

THIRTY-TWO
'Powder' shot taffeta
pleated dress with lace
embroidered dickey.
MODEL: SHALOM HARLOW

THIRTY-THREE
Short dress with wide
black lace patchwork
sleeves.
MODEL: JULIA
SCHÖNBERG

THIRTY-FOUR
Black cloqué organza
sleeveless A-line dress
embroidered with
pleated ribbons and
floral medallions.
MODEL: FLORENCE
VENTURI

THIRTY-FIVE
Short black lace kick-
pleated dress with
Arlesienne fichu effect.
MODEL: VICTORIA
HERNANDO

THIRTY-SIX
Short black lace dress
with 'knife-pleat' ruffles
caught with a pink
organza bouquet.
MODEL: AMBER
VALLETTA

THIRTY-SEVEN
Oyster and turquoise
shot taffeta cross-over
bolero with pastel flower
embroidery. Cream
chiffon romper-dress
over iridescent gold
swimsuit.
MODEL: SONIA COLE

THIRTY-EIGHT
Pastel flower organza
frock-coat with
embroidered raw silk
dickey. Wide 'banana'
crêpe pants.
MODEL: CARLA BRUNI

THIRTY-NINE
Draped low-neck white
crêpe sheath dress with
giant 'parrot-tulips'.
MODEL: SUZANNE VON
ACHINGER

FORTY
Pearl-grey satin sheath
dress with cross-over
black satin shoulder
straps, pleated back
and lace kick-pleat.
MODEL: SHALOM HARLOW

FORTY-ONE
Ruffled black organza
sheath dress.
MODEL: VICTORIA
HERNANDO

FORTY-TWO
Vermilion crêpon
chiffon 'Directoire style'
sheath dress.
MODEL: EMMA SJÖBERG

FORTY-THREE
Navy satin chiffon
'Directoire-style'
sheath dress.
MODEL: KAREN MULDER

FORTY-FOUR
Draped black chiffon
bodice top. Black piqué
skirt with orange lace
hem belted with
multicolour floral silk.
MODEL: JULIA
SCHÖNBERG

FORTY-FIVE
Handwoven black silk
knit sweater.
Ecru taffeta skirt hand-
painted with
multicolour bouquet.
MODEL: CARLA BRUNI

FORTY-SIX
'Oatmeal' tulle sheath
dress with medallion
embroidered draped
bodice opening over lace
and chiffon jumpsuit.
MODEL: AMBER
VALLETTA

FORTY-SEVEN
Embroidered
handwoven 'oatmeal'
knit 'twin-set'.
Full 'sand' figured
gazar skirt with
embroidered belt.
MODEL: FLORENCE
VENTURI

FORTY-EIGHT
Short Provençal
festoon-embroidered
orange and blue tartan
jacket. Ecru lace and
crêpe georgette
Arlesienne blouse. Full
green 'tartan' taffeta
skirt over purple 'chain'
petticoat belted with
multicolour floral silk.
MODEL: ANNA BAYLE

FORTY-NINE
Pearl-medallion-
embroidered black
floral brocade bolero-
spencer with 'puff'
sleeves. High-waisted
pastel striped pleated
taffeta dress opening
over black lace
jumpsuit.
MODEL: KATOUCHA

FIFTY
Gem-embroidered pastel
floral damask
patchwork busk dress
and 'gingham' taffeta
skirt with iridescent
lace, birds, butterflies
and embroidered
bouquet appliqués.
MODEL: SUZANNE VON
ACHINGER

FIFTY-ONE
Flower-incrusted white
Provençal piqué girdle-
jacket over white
broderie-anglaise,
guipure and lace
patchwork dress.
MODEL: EVE SALVAIL

CENTRE
PHOTOGRAPH:
The end of the show.
Christian Lacroix
with Suzanne von
Achinger and
Eve Salvail.

Lacroix: Return of the Native

In these times of sound and fury it is sometimes good to go back to our landmarks; and among the things we loved, eight or ten years ago, some 'invariables' remain. We always rediscover these elements – tiny details, a certain way of doing things, the rough sketch of an allure, even a new behaviour pattern – with the same pleasure. That same feeling of here-and-now. And why should we repress the notes of a favourite song (France, the South, the late 18th century, the Liberation, London in the sixties, or the Madrid of the movida)? Especially when they come back to the starting point with new variations on that unique theme: Haute-Couture. There's no doubt at all that those who love will follow!

Q: For several seasons, you have played at being the good pupil, proving you're not afraid of a certain classicism . . . Your new collection gives every appearance of being a joyful return to your inspirational origins.
C.L.: I shall always insist on the right to shock. Even if this sometimes means being disliked. Let's not forget Baudelaire's advice: 'Strangeness is the essential flavour in any beauty'. It's this break in the straight thread of couture that introduces this 'here-and-now' quality. But even though we break away, something constant will always remain.

Q: Aren't you afraid of going over the top and becoming vulgar?
C.L.: One of Proust's characters, a little lady trying to 'social-climb', always dressed in black, 'because one can never be vulgar in black'. In kitsch there is a lot of irreverent mockery, like the spontaneity in popular street fashion, which is a reaction against daily ugliness. There's a kind of sincerity there which I prefer to conventional chic. Provocation, which these days simply means any kind of individuality, even brazen vulgarity, is a response to the banality of everyday life, its total absence of aesthetics.

Q: But how is this translated in your work?
C.L.: For next summer, I wanted to return to some of my excesses, which I really had no reason to curb – mixtures of materials, prints, woven fabrics, colours, borrowed directly from street culture – a cross-bred look, devoid of the taboos of so-called good taste. All intermingled with a strong element of Directoire-style: a time when the finery of princesses, inclining as it did towards the clothing of shepherdesses, managed to combine a luxurious appearance with a certain free-and-easiness.

Q: Yet still remaining couture?

C.L.: Scalloping, braiding, ruffles, unlined jackets, hundreds of hours of work that cannot be seen but that always dazzle! . . . Do I need to repeat that none of these clothes is imaginable outside a couture workshop? In these violent and desperate times, the only salvation lies in sincerity and a total loyalty towards one's passions. Couture is my passion.

LINE
Suspended or long and drawn-out with disproportioned effects.

MATERIALS
Crêpes, satins and chiffon. Metallic-look leathers. Wild silks. Hand-crafted tweeds and knitwear. Men's fabrics. Lace and guipure. 18th-century fabrics. Rustic taffeta.

JEWELRY AND ACCESSORIES
Iridescent gems. Nostalgic necklaces and chokers. Corals, ceramics and volcanic stones. Hearts, crosses and flowers.

SHAPES
'Composites'. Spencers/cardigans or frock-coats. Shorts, shaped skirts, wide pants. Nightshirts, double-dresses and 'Directoire-style' sheath dresses. Big ball gowns, as always.

PATTERNS
Again and as always, spots, checks and stripes. The return of romantic or candy-coloured flowers. Medallions.

HATS
Caps, hair ornaments and headdresses rather than hats. Faded straw trimmed with black. Fishnet, veils and kiss curls. Berets perhaps.

COLOURS
Red, black and white. Ecrus, oatmeal and patinated pastels. Golds, silvers and sunflowers.

ORNAMENTS
Braiding, ruching and ruffles outlining the structures. Jewel-buttons once again. Straw, sequins and light embroidery. Hand-painting. 'Lingerie' effects.

SHOES AND BAGS
A preference for gold stiletto heels. Baskets, Dorothy bags and clutch purses in straw, metal and stamped leather.

Hats, gloves, jewelry, bags, tights, spectacles
CHRISTIAN LACROIX

Shoes
CHRISTIAN LACROIX
by
SIDONIE LARIZZI

Hairstyles
ALEXANDRE DE PARIS
and
DANIEL FRENNA

Make-up
Creation and colours
NAIK LE FUR

Catwalk Director
MARC SCHAEFFER

Music
LAURENT GODARD

Lighting and sound
LUMISON

Podium
BELLOIR ET JALLOT

Guide to the Scrapbooks

Every effort has been made to trace the copyright owners of images included in the scrapbooks. Any information regarding unidentified images would be welcomed by the publishers.

Sections in *italic* are translations of Christian Lacroix's handwritten notes.

Pages 6–7
Top left (page 6) and top right (page 7): From *Aus besten Kreisen*, Die bibliophiles Taschenbücher © Harenberg Kommunikation, Dortmund 1980. Photos © Staatliche Museen zu Berlin, Preussicher Kulturbesitz, Kunstbibliothek.

Page 8
To suggest old imitation jewelry, we will use the same technique as for Mme X, the client with the imitation cage. For the black jacket, we are in the end going to avoid the Camembert-box cupids and replace them with flowers set off by the patches of white.

Pages 34–35
Don't lose the roots with Arles.

Early 19th century in Arles = Antiquity + Directoire = 90s.

I have never actually used this period of Provençal costume. High waist and prints.

Page 34
Left: Jacket found at the Rastro flea market in Madrid. Probably early 19th century. Perhaps theatre costume.
Photographs: Lars Nilsson.

Pages 34–35
'Anciens Monuments d'Arles en Provence'.

Page 36
Antique Arles 19th century.
1980
anti-style anti-modern anti-cliché
Anglo-Provençal dandy

transparent legs

Superimposed antique drapery and Provençal quilting
try filmy, transparent summery Provençal quilting

Bolero cf English book

Page 37
By chance au hasard on a coat hanger, while working on BAZAR with Sacha, my 18th-century waistcoat given by Mrs ------ turned up over the costume of the torero Rame, born in Barcelona. Clearly I should make it as a flared jacket in blue/beige. Mix antique Arles (19th century) with 80s zest, 19th-century flair, mannish allure from English dandies.
Lou Reed for ever
anti-style
anti-modern
anti-cliché
anti-effort
it seems that such a freedom and kind of violence needs a little bit of camp poetry and the mixture fits with the 40s I ever loved
On the opposite page is the first series of sketches, the first impulse of allure.

Top: A montage of an old bullfighter jacket and an 18th-century waistcoat in ivory embroidered silk presented by Mrs Williams of San Francisco and Lambesc, France.
Centre: The Velvet Underground. *Left to right:* Sterling Morrison, Maureen 'Moe' Tucker, Lou Reed and John Cale. At The Castle, Hollywood, 1966. Photograph © by Gerard Malanga, 1966. Reproduced here by kind permission of the photographer.
Bottom: Cover of French *Vogue*, 1939. Hat by Agnès. Illustration by Eric. Courtesy Paris *Vogue*, 1939.

Pages 38–39
Tacky fashion of TV music programmes had the same lightness and daring style.

Page 38
Unidentified painting.

Page 39
Top and bottom: Photographs by Guy Bourdin, from *Nova*, December 1972. From the book, *Nova*, compiled by David Hillman & Harri Peccinotti, edited by David Gibbs, Pavilion

Books, London, 1993. *Nova* ©
IPC Magazines Ltd.
Centre: Unidentified painting.

Page 40
first ideas for hairstyles

old-fashioned is fashionable

Montage of images taken from
Aus besten Kreisen, Die
bibliophiles Taschenbücher, ©
Harenberg Kommunikation,
Dortmund 1980. Photos ©
Staatliche Museen zu Berlin,
Preussischer Kulturbesitz,
Kunstbibliothek.

Page 41
*Directoire meets with the mid-
70s and late 80s or early 90s.
Black style joins white sheer
audacity through Lycra.*

Patra, 'The Jamaican Madonna'.
Photograph © Brad Fierce,
from *THE FACE*, December
1993.

Pages 42–43
*These three pictures are of the
same woman.*

*1800-1980-1944
1801-1981-1945
Numerologically the answer is 1
– my life number. 1 is the eternal
beginning, the tabula rasa. And
these three periods are libertarian
times following great traumas:
revolution, war and the first oil
crisis: the clock is restarted at
zero with Mitterrand, with the
'45 peace, with the Directoire. It's
logical we should want that now.
Always start again from zero
every season.*

Page 42
Photograph © Francesco
Scavullo. Used here by kind
permission of the
photographer.

Page 43
Left: Unidentified painting.
Right: From *The Private Rich: A
Family Album*, by Peter Rand and
Elizabeth Bird, Crown
Publishers, New York, 1984,
p. 148.

Page 44
*Want very couture workmanship:
pin-tucks, insertions, pleats,
jewelry, blond-lace. All that is
only possible in couture but must
keep the 90s zest*

18th-century Provençal bonnet

*lace, raised
jewels
pleats
flowers
pleats
drop waist*

18th-century Provençal bonnet.
From *En Jupon piqué et robe
d'Indienne: Costumes provençaux*,
by Michel Biehn, Editions
Jeanne Laffitte, Paris, 1987, p.
144. Original photograph by
Yves Gallois. Reproduced here
by kind permission of Michel
Biehn.

Page 45
*Juxtapose delicate prettiness
with severe fabrics*

Queen Victoria of Sweden's
morning dress, of lace, crêpe de
chine and gold flowers, made by

Anna Gröber, Vienna, 1911.
Cover image of *Kungligt Klädd,
Kungligt Mode*, Berghs Förlag,
Stockholm, 1987. Reproduced
here by kind permission of the
Royal Armoury, Stockholm,
Sweden. Photograph: Göran
Schmidt.

Page 46
Want flowery prints

Want this sort of flowing line

Page 47
*The most beautiful hats in the
whole of history, along with
those of 1910 and 1780*

Pages 46–47
Pages from an unidentified
fashion magazine, early 1940s.

Page 48
*Formal wear at the Swedish
court in 1940/1950 is a
development of the Empire
fashion (sleeves).*

Ladies from the Swedish Royal
court, 1944. Photo: Jaeger. From
Kungligt Klädd, Kungligt Mode,
Berghs Förlag, Stockholm, 1987,
p. 79. Reproduced here by kind
permission of the copyright
holder, Baron Johan
Nordenfalk, Västervik, Sweden.

Page 49
*Beware bogus punks, as stupid as
grunge. But the shoes are
interesting and the mesh
resembles Ulrika's samples in silk
and chenille. Suede – suede.
Leather – leather*

Page 49
Main photo: Photograph
© Francesco Scavullo.
Reproduced here by kind
permission of the
photographer.
Centre: Carla Bruni. Photograph
by Roxanne Lowit. Used here
by kind permission of the
photographer. This photograph
originally appeared in *Vogue*.
Bottom: Samples of weaving
from Ulrika Liljedahl.

Page 50
All the feet will be gold.

1910

Why not clogs?

Venetian shoe protected by an
overshoe (Rossimoda Private
Collection). Reconstruction of
a shoe worn by Charlemagne,
taken from an old painting.
From *Footwear*, BE-MA Editrice,
Milan, 1986. Photograph
© Museo della Calzatura,
Vigevano. Used here by kind
permission of the Museo della
Calzatura, Commune di
Vigevano.
Bottom left: Shoe design in
brocade from Sidonie Larizzi.

Page 51
*I've never seen gilded python
skin.*
Venice?
1920
tongue
stiletto
gold padding

Unidentified sandal.

Pages 52–53
Pages from the magazine *100
Idées*, Paris, n.d. Photographs:
Jean-Denis Mahn.

Page 52
*To be tried out at Le Bourget
and Baseo.*

Top left: Shalom Harlow wearing
over-the-knee socks designed
by Christian Lacroix.
Christian Lacroix's 'collants'
were made at this time by the
company Le Bourget. His Lycra
garments (as well as theatre
costumes) were sometimes
made by the workshop Baseo.
Photograph by Roxanne Lowit.
Used here by kind permission of
Miss Lowit.
Photograph also courtesy of
Miss Shalom Harlow and Elite
Agency, Paris.

Page 54
Sample of embroidery by
Lesage.

Page 55
'Gloriosa Virgo Maria Mater
Iesu'. Virgin and child, gift
from M. François Lesage to
Christian Lacroix.

Page 56
*Polish Infant Jesus: the skirt
could do for the bridal gown.
Beware of being too theatrical, too
operatic. But after all in couture
it's more important than ever to
go for what I want uninhibitedly
and without self-censorship.*

*Look for the books of ex-votos
and the Saint Sulpice devotional*

*images that combine lace and
bright colours.*

Image of the Infant Jesus,
Polish.

Page 57
[Concealed by picture]
*I still like its look of old
lingerie and lace hearts. Cf.
bridal gown bodice, the
collection, why not!*

'Consummatum est'.
Montage of images from *Un
Siècle d'images de piété* (Exhibition
catalogue), Musée Galerie de la
Seita, 1984.

Page 58
*The form, disproportion and
mixing of the fabrics are
bang up to date. Don't delay
in giving old documents to
Evelyne.*
*Weaving by Anne Corbière
based on a scarf picked up in
the Portobello in September*

Examples of 18th-century male
costume.
From *Common Threads: A Parade
of American Clothing*, by Lee
Hall, Bulfinch Press, New York,
1992.
Used here by permission of
the Smithsonian Institution,
Division of Social History
(costume collection),
Washington D.C.

Page 59
gold lamé = masculine

*Just like old sun umbrellas left
out on deck in the sun in the 50s*

Anne Corbière's handwoven sample in striped silk from a shawl (Moroccan or Eastern) found in the Portobello Market, London.

Page 60
IX 93
ideas for choice of fabric

Taffetas
Warp
Reds
Yellow

Bucol
Chocolate, sunflower, vermilion, claret, sulphur, light navy, purple range
(Georgette)
pastellissime, black, navy in (satin dupion)
and in pleated dupion
fragmented effects
dupion: navy, black, mustard, purplish colour
Range of colours

Starting point for the range chosen instinctively: want acid pastels and rather faded, worn, bright colours.

Page 61
Darquer
lace; Beauclère prints

Looks like African bamboo motifs
Exclusives. Be careful no one else has them.

Finally, no.

Page 62
October. Discovered the style of 40s tweed we wanted.

Liberation feel.
Dormeuil

very pretty checks + gold – light

Fabrics from Gamma Seta and Dormeuil.

Page 63
To combine with leather and sequins
Cardigan of an Incroyable
ABS
Navy (Aral)
Cardigans without
without linings

Top left and right: Medieval costumes. Photographs copyright © Robert Basset, Musée des Tissus de Lyon.
Remaining images: Fabrics from ABS and Malhia.

Page 64
Want to put a black velvet cross over the white dresses, which look too much like romantic lingerie. (Find a more summery material.) Still and always Death in Venice, the tulle and satin creations of the heroines of 1914 and La Nave Va. Play up the rather unexpected juxtapositions. Lightweight embroideries which we should be able to leave unlined (impossible for clients). Look at more recent pictures (Variétés, Maritié and Gilbert Carpentier on Canal Jimmy). The disco dresses in Dalida. Flowing lines, a bit cheap, sequins, tying in both with forties historical reconstructions, tango dresses and those for Irene Castle, 1917, and, of course, the Merveilleuses of the Palais Royal in 1800.

Pages 64–65
Main photograph: From *The Private Rich: A Family Album*, by Peter Rand and Elizabeth Bird, Crown Publishers, New York, 1984, p. 109.
Main photograph: Head of right-hand figure: Stella Tennant. This photograph used by kind permission of Miss Tennant and Mr Mahdhi Saïf, Marilyn Agency, Paris.

Page 65
Top: Feathers from the house of Lemarié.
Centre right: Shalom Harlow. Courtesy Miss Harlow and Elite Agency Paris. Photograph by Roxanne Lowit. Used here by kind permission of the photographer. This photograph originally appeared in *Vogue.*

Page 66
Look at more recent pictures of gypsies and Spain. Look again at books of photos bought in the 80s, like Scavullo. Those years have now acquired a historical patina. We have found some good new men's fabrics (Gandini, Dormeuil and Holland & Sherry): 75ish designs for dandies of the 1930s or the 18th century (not Beauclère).
Silver representational jewelry from Panama.

Jewelry. From *Gold und Silber* by Günther Hartmann, Dietrich Reimer Verlag, Berlin, 1988. Photographs copyright © Staatliche Museen zu Berlin, Preussischer Kulturbesitz, Kunstbibliothek.

Page 67
Photo by Terry O'Neill too

Main photograph: Photograph by Michel Dieuzaide. From . . . *être Flamenco* by Michel Dieuzaide, preface by Edgar Morin, Juillard, Paris, 1992. Used here by kind permission of the publisher and the photographer.
Bottom right: Christian Lacroix with Florence.
Photograph: Lars Nilsson.

Page 68
Seen at the Metropolitan Museum, New York, on the way out of the exhibition of the show staged by American designers at Versailles in 1973: 3 absolutely tiny busts in the shape of an 1880s hourglass. Seen close up, you realize they are made of jersey knit with borders and sides and everything all embroidered with jet. Extraordinary. Idea of doing something with Danièle Boutard in Racine silk jersey to be embroidered with flowers (Lizbeth?) like cheap sweaters. China, 13th century.

Bottom: Sample of embroidered leaf by the house of Lizbeth, Paris.

Page 69
Knit + lace and embroidery
bodice
skirt?
lace?
chiffon?
pleats?

Page 70
Unidentified photograph of motor-cycle racing driver.

Page 71
Pages from *Le Patchwork: Ou la désobéissance*, by Claude Fauque and Marie-Noëlle Bayard. Syros, Paris, 1994. Photographs © UFAC (Union française des arts du costume) 107 rue de Rivoli, 75002 Paris. Used here by kind permission of the publisher and UFAC.

Page 72
Top: Unidentified photograph. *Centre:* Late-18th-century peasant dress. From *En Jupon piqué et robe d'Indienne: Costumes provençaux*, by Michel Biehn, Editions Jeanne Laffitte, Paris, 1987, p. 87. Original photograph by Yves Gallois. Reproduced here by kind permission of Michel Biehn.
Bottom: Unidentified photograph.

Page 81
green
orange
pink
shiny thread or Lycra
mini shirt
velcro fastening

Page 82
The very first proper designs; play on the disproportions

Beginning of November
Spanish jacket
summer dress
lace
front detail
+ short

The Andalusian jacket is reduced to a bolero and the tie blouse lengthens into a tunic dress over a skirt (or?)

The drawing was done before seeing the Gamma Seta collection of printed fabrics. The perfect match is a good sign, which I like.

Page 83
Drawn the same day. 1980 flowery prints.

Incroyable's silk shirt, 1930.
flower
lightweight wool
uneven pleats
Incroyable detail
handkerchief

Combine with 40s tweed in 18th-century forms playing on the wrong proportions.

Stuck in here by mistake: put back to before the journey to the USA.

Pages 84–85
I don't know why I have changed my way of drawing (line, direction faced and overall look)

Menkes quiff
hairslide
mini-hairnet
18th-century blazer, destructured, restructured tennis trousers, 1930
18th-century brocade Adidas 1930s/18th-century tennis blazer.

Pseudo Spanish hairstyle. Adidas in flowered fabric.
cut-down scarf
Flamenco
silk
chiffon

Black lace boots
Try to make transparent quilting
(. . . of the muslin too)

striped shirt, collar with white
lines
waistcoat
embroidered scarf
Rasta Couture
Want boyish jackets with a new
masculine feel rather like Guy
Bourdin

These drawings too go back to the
beginning of November.

Page 85
Centre: Unidentified photograph.

Page 86
gold mesh lace
white dress-suit jacket
stilettoes
Want clothes all in white, easy fit
but cut a little skimpily, and
stiletto heels. Gold mesh,
embroidered tights and pleated
skirts.

Pseudo-Spanish, 30s
Make it all much more fluid and
develop the Spanish dresses to
something nearer pre-war
ballgowns. Profusion of flounces
flowing to the ground.

Page 87
tailored jacket over dress
blouse underneath dress
sporty skirt under dress
Follow the pencil line for the
drapery: blouse = dress = jacket
= coat. Skirt = shorts. Checks
and flowers.

tie-collar
back
matt and shiny

18th-century asymmetrical
blouse
lace mini-skirt underneath and
pareu in uneven pleats of
georgette
Cut down the jackets and
complicate with fake historical
detail. The blouses should be
capable of being sold as dresses.
Play up the transparent layers.

Page 88
Homage to Freddie Mercury
Homage to Freddie Mercury –
bright vest, embroidered or not,
over faintly military/majorette
trousers

Cropped vest/blouse 1900,
transparent
skimpy 1900s-style garments
(skirts)

Page 89
Provençal lace
Show structural details that have
nothing to do with the actual
construction: couture = artifice

18th-century jacket, loose
pleated organza
jewel
stretch fabric or supple leather
short skirt/shorts
mules

Pages 90–91
Rediscover the fluidity of 1975.
Halston was the most amazing at
the Metropolitan (red outfit, lots
of red)

Make dresses of cut-out print
patches: go from large flowers to
small, from small flowers to spots,
from spots to lace (with the help
of Swiss muslin?)

strappy necklace
jewel
. . .
40s tweed
flowers = gold lace/combination
stiletto
little hat
shaped jacket
high-waisted trousers
Venetian lace
arrangement of patchwork
lace or Swiss muslin = spots,
small flowers
front
back
low scooped back

Page 91
[Concealed by sketches]
This kind of undergarment
should be one of the running
themes: shiny cropped vest top,
shorts. Romantic accessories . . .

Page 92
smocked neckline with shawl
effect – add a black lace scarf

Centre left: Working-class dress,
c. 1880. From *En Jupon piqué et*
robe d'Indienne: Costumes
provençaux, by Michel Biehn,
Editions Jeanne Laffitte, Paris,
1987, p. 112. Original
photograph by Gérard Poujol.
Reproduced here by kind
permission of Michel Biehn.
Centre right: Detail of *De Mina*,
by Carl Larsson, 1892. Private
collection. By kind permission
of the owner.
Bottom: Detail of *robe à la*
française, English, *c.* 1760; silk
taffeta, self-fabric trim, double
flounced cuffs. Stomacher with
bands: linen with scroll

embroidery in silk thread. Engageantes: cotton drawnwork. Fichu: recreated from 18th-century lace. From *Revolution in Fashion, 1715–1815*, by Jean Starobinski *et al.*, Abbeville Press, New York, 1989, p. 45. Used here courtesy of The Kyoto Costume Institute. Photograph by Toru Kogure, used here by kind permission of the photographer and Creators Management Studio White, Tokyo.

Page 93
spots = (flowers?) = lace patchwork

Page 94
This cross is a sign not to let slip (cf jacket on the cover of Vogue). Use it for a T-shirt under a white jacket.

Something of Gustave Moreau and Delacroix: winter in summer, the baroque and the sacred, to balance the most elemental things/ sport.

Top: Detail from *Cleopatra and the Countryman* by EugèneDelacroix, 1838. The William Hayes Ackland Memorial Art Center, Chicago.
Centre: Velvet hand-painted and block-printed sample by Sabina Fay Braxton.

Page 95
Fabric sample from Sabina Fay Braxton.

Page 96
Use linings as little as possible for suits to preserve the flowing line and texture of the material: find ways of using the internal features as a form of decoration. Pay less attention than usual to transparency, matching necklines, all that excessive formality that weighs down couture and cuts it off from the age. But no room for anything of destroy.

Fabric samples from Abraham, Taroni and Gandini.

Page 97
We are focusing on this mix and match of prints and woven cloth. Each season we approach the collection in a different way: this time there was a narrower and more coherent choice of fabrics, and the fabric was identified earlier with the first drawings, which themselves did not go off in so many different directions. Even so, it's hard to take the plunge as far as choosing the forms is concerned, and the first allocations of fabrics. I had the impression I had fewer than usual but in the end there will be the same waste of time worrying, eliminating drawings, not having a spot for fabrics one has liked for a month. As in the last two seasons, on the right-hand side there is the pile of sketches chosen, and on the left, those held in reserve.

Fabric samples from Dormeuil, Gamma Seta and Bucol.

Page 98
I want to use white.
But in the end we aren't going to manage it: no suitable fabric: the see-through ones with seams are not that interesting, piqué looks too like prêt-à-porter, grain de poudre is too masculine. What is Tom Wolfe in? I am disappointed with white, I don't really like it much.
Etienne Roda-Gil

Top left: Angie Dickinson in the film *Even Cowgirls Get the Blues*, 1993.
"Even Cowgirls Get the Blues" Copyright 1994, New Line Productions, Inc. All rights reserved. Photo by Abigail Tarsches. Photo appears courtesy of New Line Productions, Inc.
Bottom centre: 'Ballade en Blanc' by Etienne Roda-Gil.
Bottom left: Photograph of Frank Zappa. Photographer unknown.

Page 99
Main picture: Tom Wolfe by D. Fineman/Sygma.
Head shot of Tom Wolfe. Courtesy Outline/Katz.

Page 100
Beauclère

Right, top to bottom: Fabrics by Beauclère.

Page 101
More signs: found in different newspapers these two or three photos of Pierre and Gilles, very Directoire, with the look I love.

Pages 100–101
Photographs by Pierre and Gilles. Used by kind permission of the artists.

Page 102
mock 'little girl' dolly frills everywhere
beret/curl
with or without sleeves
short or long?
Want a very girlish, romantic doll look, rather 70s. The embroidery requested from Lesage is perfect for this theme.

Bottom left: Sample of embroidery from Lesage.

Page 103
Lesage
poncho batwing sleeves
corset-front effect
document
cut off or not
I had not realized the similarity between this drawing and the dress provided by Florence. Another good omen. For Lesage to embroider.

Top: Tea gown, *c.* 1907, found in a Budapest flea market. Photograph: Lars Nilsson. *Centre:* Embroidery by Lesage. *Bottom:* Turn-of-the-century white organdy baby's dress found in the Camargue, recently presented to Inès de la Fressange d'Urso's daughter. Photograph: Lars Nilsson.

Page 104
Materials that are too much like furnishing fabrics will be mixed with the very Sesame Street type

flowers from the Lanel embroidery collection, above. With black?
Really great painting on fabric gives it the pattern shown here, for making a skirt

Page 117
First fitting is reassuring, a big boost: tweed + taffeta braiding and lace with men's trousers and a pullover to be knitted by Mme Hein.

Below centre: Early 19th-century jacket in white linen with low stand-up collar. Pockets and lapels edge in blue silk ribbon. On back, pockets and collar, a flower motif is embroidered in black silk. From *Folkdräkter* by Anna-Maja Nylén, Nordiska Museet, Stockholm, 1971. Photograph: Ulla Wåger. Used here by kind permission of Nordiska Museet, Stockholm.

This page shows the progress from the real Swedish uniform to the toile. Model: Victoria. Photographs: Lars Nilsson.

Page 118
A new Madame Récamier in the style embarked upon

Aileen Mehle, also known as Suzy, columnist for *Women's Wear Daily*. Used here by kind permission of Miss Mehle.

Page 119
Weekend encounter. Monika dressed as the Tsarina.

What could be better than a late 18th-century frock-coat?

Top: Christian Lacroix with Signora Monika Soszynska-Passera.
Photograph: Lars Nilsson.
Bottom: Unidentified painting.

Page 120
Ulrika Liljedahl's sample of gold sequins, from which a skirt was made.

Page 121
A chance encounter between Ulrika's samples of gold sequins and a silk pullover – to go under a jacket that looks too 1890s, which we need from Madame Jeannine. In the end, knit with sequins is a bit routine; we will add a lamé organza top embroidered with gold flowers.

Bottom: It was debated whether a plain classic beige sweater would fit with the golden skirt. Photographs: Lars Nilsson.

Page 122
Anything can be printed or transferred onto glove leather. And Christy onto the T-shirts. More and more like the Holy Madonna. (But she won't in fact be in Paris.)

Top: Piece of purple suede with test of transfer print by Sabina Fay Braxton.
Bottom: Christy Turlington. Photograph used here by kind permission of Miss Turlington and Ford, New York.

Page 123
'Les Pivoines' (Peonies), 1993. Photograph by Don Freeman.

Used by kind permission of the photographer.

Page 124
Urgent to get started with the bags because of the fifth week of holiday over Christmas, and the show coming earlier.
You never design better than when the collection has found its dynamic and you are under pressure, for you go straight to the essentials; straw and embossed leather, weaving and basketwork in metal with trim . . . have it wrapped round with gold lamé taffeta.

Top: Basketwork.
Photograph: Lars Nilsson.

Page 125
Ulrika shoulder strap
Lumen
+ leather of fabric trompe-l'oeil basket, Lemarié velvet and wicker
Lumen

strap
Lumen
Sabina
double handle
lace
Ulrika Rabanne
velvet

Corbière or Ulrika

Page 126
The most beautiful shot taffetas of the season. No qualms about having them embroidered by Lesage as long as there is a satin slip and gold body underneath Hard to choose the patches, combining taffeta and wool +

ruching in three colours.

Top: Effect of mixture of taffetas and embroidery.
Photographs: Lars Nilsson.
Bottom: Effect of ruffles on checked jacket.
Photographs: Lars Nilsson.

Page 127
In the end the bride will have a peasanty look. Replace the original slipover with an overdose of lace, brocade and 18th-century embroidered satin Gschadt Goya

Top: Fitting of 18th-century corset on Suzanne.
Photographs: Lars Nilsson.
Bottom: Fitting for a kind of dirndl inspired by a Swedish 18th-century skirt. On Suzanne.
Photographs: Lars Nilsson.

Page 128
22 or 23 XII/93
We have found good lattice motifs in lace for the underbodice of the Arlesienne of 1900.

Top: Queen Victoria of Sweden's morning dress, of lace, crêpe de chine and gold flowers, made by Anna Gröber, Vienna, 1911. Cover image of *Kungligt Klädd, Kungligt Mode,* Berghs Förlag, Stockholm, 1987. Used here by kind permission of the Royal Armoury, Stockholm.
Photograph: Göran Schmidt.
Bottom: Effect of lace on mannequin.

Page 129
Revival of 80s spots. It works. The bra underneath will become a separate lace dress. Revival too of the 'pouf' of 87.

Fittings. On Victoria.
Photographs: Lars Nilsson.

Page 130
23 or 24 XII 93
2 little black dresses are created

strapped blouse
flower
pleated flounce +

Page 131
striped tulle
double strap
flowered tulle
black flowers
Lemarié ruching
stripes + working
Lemarié organza
lace, raised
jewels
pleats
flowers
pleats
drop waist

I love this kind of puzzle where, using all the ingredients available, you struggle to create the initial design, which itself takes no account of reality.

Pages 130–131
Bottom: Sample cards from Forster Willi and Lemarié.

Page 131
On the hanger: Turn-of-the-century baby's dress in white organdy.
Photograph: Lars Nilsson.

Page 132
24/XII 93
Like a sort of turtle dove for sale in a proper bridal gown. Almost like a sample card from Forster.

Page 133
cap?

But must find a way of having the same look as the rest of the collection, something out of step, one leg sticking out. Why not a cap?

Page 134
24 December 93
Jean-Jacques has had the idea of using drapes for the set at the Inter-Continental this year, rather than plants. See the books on Bérard and O. Messel. Ask Michael for faille that rustles, as in the pictures.

Top: Sketch of the stage.

Page 135
Last Sunday Françoise wrote the poem for the invitation card, which is printed.

Invitation card, with poem by Françoise Lacroix.

Page 136
Last season or past days results or indications can't become any rule or law for the next season's behaviours.

Page 137
23 or 24/XII/93
Jacket a success. Embroider it? Gold if it is possible to give the

impression the straw colour is part of the weave. Underneath? Velcro mini-purse.

The last models left to decide on. The fabrics are a perfect match. The sequins the first to go, along with the exclusive lace, also forgotten. Keep the idea of embroidery.

Top right: Fitting on Florence. Photograph: Lars Nilsson.
Right: Samples of striped cotton by Guillemin.
Bottom right: Sequins by Jakob Schlaepfer.
Left: Lace from Gamma Seta.

Page 138
24/XII 93
Keep the original pompon at the tips of the collar, red/yellow

Bottom: Andalusian pants/pareu. dress fabric Holland + Sherry.

Page 139
27/XII 93
The freedom of others extends my freedom infinitely – Bakunin Good deed of the day: do the collage of flowers.

and put the 'Chinese' flowers for Lizbeth on Danièle's 1880s corset

Top: Effect of positioning of photocopy of embroideries on a silk jersey cardigan, then in pattern cloth.
Bottom left and right: Toile of a dress after being made in calque paper for placement of flowers. Photographs: Lars Nilsson.

Page 140
Jan[e] Austen in Arles! Menendez Brothers embroidery

Top centre: Sample of toile de Jouy from Lelièvre.
Top and bottom: Fitting for a Lesage embroidery on Victoria. Photographs: Lars Nilsson.

Page 141
Arlesienne costume. From *Histoire du Costume d'Arles*, by Odile and Magali Pascal, 1992. Photograph: Bernard Terlay, Musée Granet, Aix en Provence. Textiles: Private Collection.

Page 142
Top left: From *The Private Rich: A Family Album*, by Peter Rand and Elizabeth Bird, Crown Publishers, New York, 1984, p. 148.
Other pictures show the point at which the right mixture of pattern was found for making the outfit.
Below left: Monika Soszynska-Passera.
Photograph: Lars Nilsson.

Page 143
40s prints. In the end we'll combine the 2 Ghioldis (the stripes and the rows of Provençal motifs) in the same outfit (the 40s pyjamas) with a top in flowered fabric – try Ulrika's Directoire mini-jersey. The second dress planned with this Liberation feel will be replaced by a second plain-coloured sheath dress that is in the spirit of red. Seek the form

and find the right colour to match it.

Ulrika

Top right: Sample from Ulrika Liljedahl.

Page 144
The 'cartoon' patchwork is done at last

Collage of photocopies of different patterns of flowers from Beauclère made for the patchwork of the dress shown *centre right* (and seen in paper on p. 139).
Photograph of dress: Lars Nilsson.

Page 145
Pleated tennis skirt – white – or silver or platinum quilted leather skirt. Definitely metallic Lycra body.

Right: Fittings on Florence of the checked jacket (see p. 126, *bottom*), with addition of silver Pantone to see what effect a leather skirt would make.
Photographs: Lars Nilsson.

Page 146
29/XII 93
Handbag in maribou and ruffed ostrich

bag made of feathers
shawl
bamboo
Lumen
shawl
bamboo
Lumen

sunshade with Spanish shawl; bamboo handle + light (Mantos de Manilla) Lumen

Page 147
30/XII 93
Following pages: work with Lesage. Everything is under way at his end

Must decide as fast as possible everything from Lemarié (feathers, flowers) and find 1984 bouquets.

Centre: Cover of *Marie Claire*, 1930s/1940s. Used here by kind permission of *Marie Claire*.
Photograph: Saad.
Other pictures: Samples from the house of Lemarié.

Page 148
Collage for gloves

Page 149
Collage for gloves

Design used by kind permission of Paul McCartney.

Page 150
31/XII 93
Hand over the last sketches

Last morning of the year. Last homage (came later) to Louise de Vilmorin and her 1948 long kilts, stoles and Victorian blouses.

Last appearance: the forgotten bronze lace by Jakob Schlaepfer is perfect for the bridal gown (underskirt)

Fittings on Suzanne.
Photographs: Lars Nilsson.

Page 151
Photograph of Louise de Vilmorin, from *Point de Vue*, Paris. Courtesy: Gerard Wurtz/Gamma.

Page 152
2/I 94
Don't be afraid of making very historical head ornaments combined with plaits, brooches, débutante's feathers, bows, trims, jewelry, even lace. To counterbalance with something very sporty.

Suzanne watching Suzanne watching Suzanne

Effect of 'Josephine' hairstyles.
Model: Suzanne.
Photographs: Lars Nilsson.

Page 153
1936 boater trimmed with black Satin + trimming (Ulrika) bow?
straw hat to be aged by Caraco and trimmed

Right: The Little Fourteen-Year-Old Dancer, by Edgar Degas, 1879-81. Collection Mr and Mrs Paul Mellon, Upperville, Virginia, USA.
Top centre and bottom centre: Jean-Luc Evrard, Christian Lacroix's assistant on Ready-to-Wear accessories.
Photographs: Lars Nilsson.
Top left: Fitting on Florence.
Photograph: Lars Nilsson.
Other pictures: Fittings on Monika Soszynska-Passera.
Photographs: Lars Nilsson.

Page 154
The feathers are perfect with the enamelled Hurel brooch and with all the colours of the bridal outfit.

Right: Old pale effect of feathers on old pale straw hats with addition of golden Pantone.
Left: Fitting of 18th-century dress on Suzanne.
Photographs: Lars Nilsson.

Page 155
jewellery, oxidized old gold, Cécile dress (imitating wrought ironwork) = amethyst 'etc' in the same spirit as the picture platinum, as on the illustration. Scallops covered with iridescent embroidered lace, over-embroidered with elements of (sweet old-fashioned) edelweiss and pastel flowers (mock waistcoat)

Cécile collar in pastel

Page 156
Top left: Hat fitting on Monika Soszynska-Passera.
Photograph: Lars Nilsson.
Bottom left: From American *Vogue*, 1939. Hat by Suzy. Illustration by René Bouët-Willaumez. Courtesy American *Vogue*. Copyright © The Condé Nast Publications, Inc.
Top right: Cover of French *Vogue*, 1939. Hat by Suzy. Illustration by René Bouché. Courtesy Paris *Vogue*, 1939.
Other pictures: Unidentified painting.

Page 157
We are suffering and struggling for hats!
8.7.94

Bottom: Pablo Picasso: Design for a scarf (for the Festival mondial de la jeunesse et des étudiants par la Paix, which took place in Berlin in 1951) © Succession Picasso/DACS 1996.

Page 158
Sublime bouquets, birds and butterflies from Lesage

Top: Placement of flowers and birds embroidered by Lesage on Rubelli checked taffetas.
Main picture: Dress: *robe à la française*, French, *c.* 1760; silk taffeta plaid, self-fabric trim, double flounced cuffs. Stomacher: *échelle* in ribbon recreated from 18th-century material. Engageantes, quill and lappet: Argentan needle lace. Necklace and earrings: bubble pearls. Bracelets: bubble pearl and white paste on ribbon. Shoes: silk satin embroidered in floral chainstitch, high heels. Shoe buckles: white paste set in silver. From: *Revolution in Fashion: European Clothing, 1715–1815* by Jean Starobinski *et al.*, Abbeville Press, New York, 1989, p. 38. Used here courtesy of The Kyoto Costume Institute. Photograph by Toru Kogure, used here by kind permission of the photographer and Creators Management Studio White, Tokyo.

Page 159
Detail of Lesage embroidered bird and Rubelli checked taffeta.
Bottom: Unidentified painting.

Page 160
Something of Walt Disney's Cinderella with garlands . . .

Page 161
Cut down the top and add flowers.
40s Arlesienne
Twelfth Night.

Pages 160–161
Fittings on Suzanne, Florence and Victoria in Walt Disney Cinderella style. The silver paper crown is a French tradition: on 6 January a special cake is eaten with a china object inside. Whoever finds the object (called 'fève' [broad bean] in French because in ancient times it used to be a vegetable) is crowned King or Queen.
Photographs: Lars Nilsson.

Pages 162–163
Monday 10 January 93
We have the print of the photo of Swan Soto by A. Ch. Beau and the sample postcard from Annie Montex has got off to a good start.

Swan Soto. Photograph by Alain-Charles Beau. Reproduced here by kind permission of the photographer.

Pages 164–165
Fittings on Suzanne, Florence and Victoria.
Photographs: Lars Nilsson.

Page 165

Krivoshey's skirt looks well, elegant, lacks leaves at the back but never mind. The white bridal gown works with the cap and 'mysteries of the orient' blue corset.

Page 166

Turned round or not, with or without photographed flowers, all black and white, or coloured flowers, with or without writing, sewn or not, colour or not.

Here some exotic flowers have been added to the photograph of Swan Soto by Alain-Charles Beau (a T-shirt design) to see if this would strengthen the effect. Photographs: Lars Nilsson.

Page 167

All the mistakes or imperfections of the day (too much 41, not enough 40s, etc) should be taken as signs from the gods and kept permanently just the way they are.

Page 168

Black feathers tried out with Italian straw hats 'patinated' by Caraco.

Problem with berets

The embossed leather pockets by S.B. work with the tweed but we'll have to change the chain. Look at shorts.

Problem of body under the yellow embroidered jacket. Replace it with black lace. Problem with the ribbons too.

Top: Monika Soszynska-Passera fitting hats, painted by Christian Lacroix with silver and gold Pantone plus Tipp-Ex in mid-European 18th-century aristocratic portrait style. Photographs: Lars Nilsson. *Bottom:* Fitting on Suzanne. Photograph: Lars Nilsson.

Page 169

12/I 94

Today's mistakes are real mistakes (the flowers on the sandals). These signs from the gods we would do better to fight! Imagine a transparent body for transparency, or straps.

black tights? bare feet? natural?

Right: Fitting on Florence. Photograph: Lars Nilsson.

Pages 170–172

All photographs: Guy Marineau

Acknowledgments are owed to the following models:

Suzanne von Achinger
Anna Bayle
Carla Bruni
Sonia Cole
Shalom Harlow
Victoria Hernando
Katoucha
Karen Mulder
Eve Salvail
Julia Schönberg
Emma Sjöberg
Amber Valletta
Florence Venturi

Acknowledgments

Christian Lacroix

I should like to thank those who have generously allowed me to reproduce their work in this book:

Alain-Charles Beau
Michel Biehn
Claude Fauque and
   Marie-Noelle Bayard
Don Freeman
François Lesage
Roxanne Lowit
Marie Claire
Aileen Mehle (Suzy)
Paul McCartney
Museo della Calzatura,
   Vigevano
Odile and Magali Pascal
Pierre and Gilles
Francesco Scavullo
American *Vogue*
French *Vogue*

Gratitude is also due to the following, who kindly allowed photographs of themselves to appear here:

Suzanne von Achinger
Anna Bayle
Carla Bruni
Sonia Cole
Shalom Harlow
Victoria Hernando
Katoucha
Karen Mulder
Eve Salvail
Julia Schönberg
Emma Sjöberg
Monika Soszynska-Passera
Stella Tennant
Christy Turlington
Amber Valletta
Florence Venturi

The publishers

We should like to thank first and foremost Lars Nilsson, at Christian Lacroix, whose cooperation and generous help were invaluable. Thanks also go to the following:

Stig Anderson, Stockholm
Carl Hafström, Stockholm
Duchess Leoni of
   Amsterdam, Paris
Lorraine Mead, American
   Vogue
Baron Johan Nordenfalk,
   Västervik, Sweden
Mahdhi Saïf, Marilyn
   Agency, Paris
Peter Townsend, Sherlin
   Townsend, London
Nicole Williams, Ford, New
   York
Kelly Worts, London

Index